Economics for Lovers of Literature

Geraint Johnes

Economics for Lovers of Literature

Geraint Johnes
Lancaster University Management School
Lancaster, UK

ISBN 978-3-031-26485-6   ISBN 978-3-031-26486-3 (eBook)
https://doi.org/10.1007/978-3-031-26486-3

This Palgrave Macmillan imprint is published by the registered company Springer Nature Switzerland AG
The registered company address is: Gewerbestrasse 11, 6330 Cham, Switzerland

Preface

There's nothing like a good book. Books tell a story, yet leave gaps to be filled by the imagination of the reader. We each bring something of ourselves to the story. Often, when a book is dramatised, we watch the movie and dislike it because the characters aren't just how we imagined them to be.

When I have read some of the classics of English literature, I have viewed these through the lens of my own experience. Some of that is an experience of life that many will share, but some are more specific. In particular, there are passages in books that resonate with me because of my professional experience as an economist. Often these passages were written long before any economist came along to codify the ideas.

This book is my attempt to show how little snippets from classic works of literature have reminded me of economic ideas. In some cases the text of the novels represents ideas that were in the zeitgeist and that, albeit subconsciously, might have stimulated economic thinking at the time. In some cases the literature that has stimulated my thinking has had obvious economic content—the works of Elizabeth Gaskell or Charles Dickens, focusing as they do on poverty in the industrial heartlands, are examples. In other cases, the author of a novel might have little explicit interest in economics, but a turn of phrase might nevertheless have some power in explaining an economic concept. Thomas Hardy's work is a case in point. Indeed a major virtue of the novel as an art form is that it does more than describe what is apparent on the surface—it allows inspection of protagonists' motivations, and herein is a direct parallel to the economist's approach in which actions often follow the pursuit of objectives that may be known only to the individual. The book thus presents a broad sweep of the subject of economics, motivated by quotes taken from a broad sweep of literature. To ensure that the quotes are all taken from widely available sources, I have restricted myself to the classics—these are works of literature that are out of copyright and may be freely accessed online through sources such as Project Guthenberg. If either this book encourages the reader to read one or more of the classics, or it provokes some thinking about the underlying economics, or it conveys something about the way economists think, or if it's quite simply a book that you enjoy reading, it will have done its job.

Comments received from several people who have kindly read earlier drafts have served to improve the end product. I acknowledge in particular those of Brendan Cronin, Sue Donald, Barry Hobson, Jill Johnes, Katriana Johnes, David Philpott and many of my students, especially those in Lancaster University's MBA programme. Two anonymous referees also provided useful advice. I am grateful also to Lauren Dooley, Ellie Duncan and their teams at Palgrave whose input into the project has been immense.

Lancaster, UK   Geraint Johnes

Contents

Contents

Chapter 1
Demand and Supply—The Price of Oysters

From James Joyce: Ulysses

Yes but what about oysters. Unsightly like a clot of phlegm. Filthy shells. Devil to open them too. Who found them out? Garbage, sewage they feed on. Fizz and Red bank oysters. Effect on the sexual. Aphrodis. He was in the Red Bank this morning. Was he oysters old fish at table perhaps he young flesh in bed no June has no ar no oysters. But there are people like things high. Tainted game. Jugged hare. First catch your hare. Chinese eating eggs fifty years old, blue and green again. Dinner of thirty courses. Each dish harmless might mix inside. Idea for a poison mystery. That archduke Leopold was it no yes or was it Otto one of those Habsburgs? Or who was it used to eat the scruff off his own head? Cheapest lunch in town. Of course aristocrats, then the others copy to be in the fashion. Milly too rock oil and flour. Raw pastry I like myself. Half the catch of oysters they throw back in the sea to keep up the price. Cheap no-one would buy. Caviare. Do the grand. Hock in green glasses. Swell blowout. Lady this. Powdered bosom pearls. The élite. Crème de la crème. They want special dishes to pretend they're.

Ulysses is a humdinger of a book, probably my all-time favourite. The action takes place on an ordinary day (16 June 1904) in the life of an ordinary man (Leopold Bloom), but through his memories and thoughts it extends to cover his family's entire life history. And what a story that is! The central characters—Bloom, his wife Molly, and his friend, Stephen Dedalus—correspond to those in Homer's epic poem, the Odyssey, whose basic structure the novel also shares. Each chapter is written in a different literary style, and this leaves the reader with an impression of unevenness, adding to the often-bewildering nature of the prose that is written as a stream of consciousness. Yet, rather like the image in an almost abstract impressionist painting, the storyline emerges clearly through what initially seems to be a mass of incomprehensible gibberish and barely relevant detail. It is not the easiest book to read, but it is hugely rewarding and a massively impressive achievement. As I said, it's probably my all-time favourite—either that, or 'We're Going on a Bear Hunt'.

© The Author(s), under exclusive license to Springer Nature Switzerland AG 2023
G. Johnes, *Economics for Lovers of Literature*,
https://doi.org/10.1007/978-3-031-26486-3_1

So what determines the price of oysters? This is a puzzle that many gourmands may have pondered when eating them. From an economic perspective, there may be something a little unusual about oysters, as we shall see later, but the principle of how their price is determined is basically the same as that of how any other price comes about.

To understand prices, we need first to understand the principles of demand and supply. The demand for a product reflects a willingness and ability to pay for it. I may *desire* a Lamborghini, but if I am not willing (and able) to pay the price, I don't (in any economically meaningful sense) *demand* it. If the price of a Lamborghini were to fall (a lot), then I might become willing and able to buy one—in which case I would demand one. This is an example of demand increasing on the *extensive margin*—the price cut brings more potential buyers into the market. For other types of product, demand may also increase on the intensive margin as price falls—in this case existing buyers want to buy more. So, for example, I might want to buy more cups of coffee per day if the price were halved.

The demand for a product depends on a lot of things other than price. It depends on the nature of the product. Some products, such as water, are necessities. Others, like Lamborghinis, are luxuries. Demand also depends on income. As my income rises, so my demand might switch from budget brands to designer brands. But, for the time being at least, let's focus on the fact that, usually, demand rises as the price of the product falls.

For some products, demand is highly responsive to the price, so that a fall in the price leads to a substantial increase in the quantity that people want to buy. Or, to put it another way, an increase in the price leads to a substantial reduction in how much people want to buy. Economists refer to these types of products as having an *elastic* demand. An example of a product of this type might be meals out at a restaurant. If these become more expensive, people can readily switch to eating at home—so demand for eating out falls quite rapidly as price increases. In August 2020, during the COVID-19 pandemic, the UK government sought to encourage people to eat out by subsidising restaurant meals—and the result was a huge increase in demand on those days for which the offer was available. For some other products, for example, salt, demand is hardly responsive at all to changes in price. But for most goods, the general principle that demand is negatively related to price holds good.

There are exceptions. The above extract from James Joyce's work suggests that oysters might provide an example of demand that rises as the price goes up 'cheap, no one would buy'. There are at least two reasons why this might happen. The first concerns snob value. People might want to buy oysters because the act of doing so itself confers on them some status. It signals to other people that they can afford to buy such luxuries. Another reason is that higher prices may be perceived to be an indicator of higher quality.

The impact of snob value is apparent in many writings around the turn of the twentieth century. Edith Wharton for example, in her novel The House of Mirth, tells of the desirability of an 'unlimited effect'—what we might describe as conspicuous consumption.

Life went on through Lily's teens: a zig-zag broken course down which the family craft glided on a rapid current of amusement, tugged at by the underflow of a perpetual need—the need of more money. Lily could not recall the time when there had been money enough, and in some vague way her father seemed always to blame for the deficiency. It could certainly not be the fault of Mrs. Bart, who was spoken of by her friends as a "wonderful manager." Mrs. Bart was famous for the unlimited effect she produced on limited means; and to the lady and her acquaintances there was something heroic in living as though one were much richer than one's bank-book denoted.

Lily was naturally proud of her mother's aptitude in this line: she had been brought up in the faith that, whatever it cost, one must have a good cook, and be what Mrs. Bart called "decently dressed." Mrs. Bart's worst reproach to her husband was to ask him if he expected her to "live like a pig"; and his replying in the negative was always regarded as a justification for cabling to Paris for an extra dress or two, and telephoning to the jeweller that he might, after all, send home the turquoise bracelet which Mrs. Bart had looked at that morning.

While price is an important factor in determining the level of demand for a product, it is not the only one. Demand can shift owing to changes in taste. People demand more flowers just before Valentine's Day and more turkeys just before Christmas than at other times of the year. They demand more cold drinks and ice cream in the summer than in the winter.

Another factor that influences demand is income. For normal goods, an increase in income serves to increase demand. There are, however, some goods for which this is not the case. The demand for many dairy items and fats goes down as personal income rises; this may be because people are able to switch to consuming more expensive substitutes. Products of this type are often referred to as inferior goods. It's important to note, however, that that is not a judgement on their quality, but rather a technical description of how demand for the product varies with income. Indeed, it may be a smart move for producers to supply a mix of normal and inferior goods to the market, because this protects them against swings in demand that are due to fluctuations in income. For this reason, many supermarkets offer both premium brand and basic brand items. When things are going well, customers will switch to buying the premium brand, but if their income falls they may turn instead to the basic brand.

The demand for any particular product is also determined, in part, by the market for other products. Some things go well together—they complement each other—so that a rise in the price of one good leads to a fall in demand not only for that good but also for its complement. Fish and chips, swimwear and sunblock, IT devices and internet access are examples. Other pairs of goods are substitutes for one another, so that a rise in the price of one of the goods results in a switching of demand away from that good, and towards the other. Examples are meat and fish, movie streaming services and cinema tickets, CDs and vinyl, gold and bitcoin.[1]

---

[1] While fluctuations in the price of bitcoin have been severe, it has been held as an asset my optimistic investors.

Demand is only one part of what goes on in the market for any product. It is important also to consider supply. This concerns how much of a product its producers are willing and able to supply at any given price. As the price rises, so we would expect more producers to be attracted into the market, so supply increases at the extensive margin. We would also expect existing producers to be willing to produce more—so supply also increases at the intensive margin.

Since both demand and supply depend (in part, at least) on the price of a product, it's possible to compare the levels demanded and supplied at each price. At a very high price, demand will be low, but producers will be willing to supply a high level of output. This leads to a situation of glut—also known as an excess supply. Producers quickly find that they cannot sell all the output that they want at this price, and to get rid of the excess supply they will reduce the price. For perishable goods such as fresh fruit or meat, this happens quickly. At the end of the day, stocks might be sold off cheaply. For more durable goods the price may take longer to fall, but it still falls eventually. Consider refrigerators (or any other type of 'white goods'). A retailer might be holding on to an excess supply. This takes up warehousing space that is costly to rent. At some stage, the retailer needs to trade off the cost of this space against the financial hit taken by selling the stock at a reduced price. Eventually, the excess supply leads to downward pressure on the price.

Now consider the case of a very low price. Demand will be high, but supply will be relatively low. There is a shortage (sometimes called an excess demand). Producers will realise that they can raise the price and sell more—truly a win–win situation for them. So a shortage leads to increasing prices. Indeed, fishermen may throw some of their catch back into the sea to ensure a limited supply and high price!

Both gluts and shortages are problems that, in effect, fix themselves. Producers respond to incentives by adjusting the price so that demand and supply are brought into balance (at least roughly). It's always possible for a shock to happen and that might throw things out of balance again—but if this happens the price would once again enter this process of adjustment so as to remove any glut or shortage. Christmas might raise the demand for turkeys; if there's a shortage, the price rises. A rainy spell in August might reduce the demand for ice cream; look out for good supermarket offers.

There is a subtle joke in Joyce's ruminations about the price of oysters. Limiting supply by throwing oysters back into the sea is effective as a means of raising the price under normal circumstances. If, however, demand were to rise as the price increases, a higher price would mean increased demand, and so the fishermen will meet this by selling more oysters, not by throwing back surplus catch. (Otherwise the excess demand would push both the price and supply up further.) So both explanations offered by Joyce cannot be right. That process of starting a thought, moving on to something else, and maybe contradicting the earlier thought is of course typical of a stream of consciousness.

We'll look at the underpinnings of demand and supply in more detail in the next few chapters. But the big message of the present chapter, as James Joyce might say, is that price depends on demand and supply.

Consider how demand and supply affect the price of essential items such as water (which has considerable value in sustaining life) and of original artwork by Leonardo da Vinci (which doesn't).

Chapter 2
Surpluses—When You've Got to Go, You've Got to Go

From Lawrence Sterne: Tristram Shandy

He the said Walter Shandy shall, at his own proper cost and charges, and out of his own proper monies, upon good and reasonable notice, which is hereby agreed to be within six weeks of her the said Elizabeth Mollineux's full reckoning, or time of supposed and computed delivery,—pay, or cause to be paid, the sum of one hundred and twenty pounds of good and lawful money, to John Dixon, and James Turner, Esqrs. or assigns,—upon TRUST and confidence, and for and unto the use and uses, intent, end, and purpose following:—That is to say,—That the said sum of one hundred and twenty pounds shall be paid into the hands of the said Elizabeth Mollineux, or to be otherwise applied by them the said Trustees, for the well and truly hiring of one coach, with able and sufficient horses, to carry and convey the body of the said Elizabeth Mollineux, and the child or children which she shall be then and there enceint and pregnant with,—unto the city of London.

The stream of consciousness style of writing is often associated with authors of the early twentieth century such as James Joyce. But a century and a half earlier, Lawrence Sterne wrote The Life and Opinions of Tristram Shandy, Gentleman— a novel that, perhaps more than any other, epitomises the style. The protagonist, Tristram Shandy, aims to write his autobiography, but is so prone to digression that he does not get very far. The digressions initially infuriate the reader, but after a while it becomes clear that they are indeed the whole point of the book. Tristram's persistent failure to stick to the point shifts from irritating to hysterical. A film starring Rob Brydon and Steve Coogan—A Cock and Bull Story—is loosely based on the book. Nothing happens in that either, but it too is very funny.

What makes a taxi ride worth £120 to the people buying it? Distance travelled might be one thing. Sterne does not tell us from where Elizabeth might have been travelling, but it may have been from Shandy Hall, and this may have been in Yorkshire—in which case the journey would have been around 240 miles. The number of passengers might be another factor. A measure of need is another.

© The Author(s), under exclusive license to Springer Nature Switzerland AG 2023
G. Johnes, *Economics for Lovers of Literature*,
https://doi.org/10.1007/978-3-031-26486-3_2

In the case described by Sterne, Elizabeth needs to get to London to give birth.
If she perceives that she can only receive adequate medical support in London, then
she will value the journey there very highly. Indeed, more generally, the utility that
people get from consuming goods and services is key to understanding how they value
these products. And that utility does not necessarily bear any relation to the costs of
providing the products. As the birth approached, Elizabeth's need became urgent,
and this likely raised her valuation of the journey to London, albeit temporarily.

For the provider of the taxi service, the costs may be quite modest. At the time
that Tristram Shandy was written, the journey might have taken two days in each
direction, and would have required payment for the driver, hire of several teams
of horses, and upkeep of the carriage itself. At that time the annual salary paid to
coachmen amounted to between £30 and £40, so the labour cost associated with
one leg of the journey might be approximated as £1. It is unlikely that the other
costs would have amounted to very much more than that. Maybe £5 would cover the
firm's costs for both legs of the journey. So £120 (even though it was also intended to
include some costs other than the taxi ride) appears to be a very generous allowance.
This is not, however, the point. We need to consider what the alternatives might have
been. There was, at the time, a regular coach service from York to London, and the
fare amounted to around £5 for a one way journey. However this service only ran
during the summer months, and using it might not have been deemed appropriate
for someone of Walter's social standing. If the alternative were for Walter to take
Elizabeth to London himself, he would have to sacrifice all sorts of other activities.
(We might very well think that he ought to have done so, but again that is not the
point.) Walter earned his living as a merchant. While merchants' incomes varied
widely, it is likely that he earned an annual income of at least £5000. Sacrificing over
a week's work and earning potential to deliver Elizabeth to and from London would
entail sacrificing a significant amount of income—perhaps around £120.

The figure that Walter is prepared to pay for the taxi ride thus comes from his
estimate of what the next best alternative would cost him—and is completely unre-
lated to the costs incurred by the taxi form. The fact that there is a gap between these
two values is important because it is what makes trade worthwhile. In the same way,
I hire a decorator to work on my house; I could do the work myself, but my time
would better be used on other things. Likewise I sometimes go to a restaurant or get
a takeaway meal; I could cook the food myself, but I find the idea of paying someone
else to do it once in a while appealing—so long as I pay them less than the value I
put on my time. Fortunately, they find that this is a good deal for them too, because
they value the income that they can earn in by decorating or cooking for me more
highly than they value spending their time on other things. These differences in how
people value things allow goods and services to be exchanged—since the trades are
entirely voluntary, it must be the case that both parties gain. If Walter were to pay
£120 for a taxi ride, he would almost certainly be paying a good deal more than it
costs the taxi company to provide the service; but he would nevertheless be paying it
willingly, and the ride would be providing him with (at least) £120 worth of utility.
The taxi company, meanwhile, would also be profiting from the deal.

As a result of Walter exploiting a loophole in his marriage settlement, his son Tristram was born with a flat nose. Yes, really. It seems that Walter was not as keen to part with £120 as a cursory reading of the settlement would imply, and that had complex consequences. Tristram was not Walter and Elizabeth's first born—Tristram's brother Bobby was already at school when Tristram arrived. Perhaps Walter valued subsequent children somewhat less highly than his first. That does not reflect well on him, but it does serve to illustrate a principle that is familiar to economists—simply put, the less one has of something, the more one values it.

Imagine that you are in a sushi bar and the dishes, each of which is priced at £2, are coming past you on a conveyor belt. When you first arrive, you are very hungry. You might be prepared to pay £10 for your first dish. The price of £2 seems a very good deal (and is a price that you are very willing to pay, while enjoying an £8 surplus!). After eating it, you might still be hungry, and might be prepared to pay as much as £5 for your second dish; of course it would only cost you £2 and you would enjoy £3 worth of utility as a surplus. By now though, you are starting to get full. Nevertheless you would be willing to pay £2 for a third dish—so you do. After that, you might be willing to pay just £1 for a fourth dish—but since the fourth dish would cost you £2 you decide not to be so greedy. The principle that the utility you get from the last unit that you consume tends to fall as you consume more serves to tell you how much you should consume—in this case just three dishes. The demand that an individual has for a product is thus determined by the utility that the product gives the individual. And the aggregate demand for the product is the sum of demand across all individuals. Demand is underpinned by utility.

Since both parties to a trade gain from the trade, it follows that trade is good. If Walter and the taxi company were to agree on a fare of £100, it is possible to measure the gain that each makes. We know that Walter would be prepared to pay as much as £120, so he must be enjoying a surplus of £20 as a result of the trade. Meanwhile, the taxi firm might have costs of £5 and hence earn a profit of £95 from the deal. Both of these surpluses—Walter's surplus of £20 and the firm's surplus of £95—represent benefits that arise from the trade. Neither party to the trade needed to earn these surpluses to make the trade worthwhile for them, but they receive the surpluses anyway. They are like rabbits pulled out of a hat—economic welfare that arises as if by magic, simply because people trade with each other. Making the most of these surpluses seems to be a very worthwhile endeavour. With very few exceptions, we can conclude that trade is good, and anything that interferes with trade is bad.

In the example that we have considered here, the taxi firm makes a substantial profit. Where large profits can be earned so easily, it seems reasonable to expect that new firms may be set up to try to compete with the existing provider. Where the incumbent charges £100 and makes a profit of £95, a new firm might try to undercut the price and take the custom. The impact of this type of competition forms the economic focus of the next couple of chapters.

Consider a maintenance job on your home—something like changing a washer in a tap, fitting some kitchen units, or decorating the living room. What light do the ideas in this chapter throw on your choice of whether to undertake the task yourself or to hire a tradesperson to do the job?

Chapter 3
Perfect Competition—The Competition's Tough

From Charles Dickens: A Tale of Two Cities

It could scarcely be called a trade, in spite of his favourite description of himself as "a honest tradesman." His stock consisted of a wooden stool, made out of a broken-backed chair cut down, which stool, young Jerry, walking at his father's side, carried every morning to beneath the banking-house window that was nearest Temple Bar: where, with the addition of the first handful of straw that could be gleaned from any passing vehicle to keep the cold and wet from the odd-job-man's feet, it formed the encampment for the day. On this post of his, Mr. Cruncher was as well known to Fleet-street and the Temple, as the Bar itself,—and was almost as in-looking.

Encamped at a quarter before nine, in good time to touch his three-cornered hat to the oldest of men as they passed in to Tellson's, Jerry took up his station on this windy March morning, with young Jerry standing by him, when not engaged in making forays through the Bar, to inflict bodily and mental injuries of an acute description on passing boys who were small enough for his amiable purpose. Father and son, extremely like each other, looking silently on at the morning traffic in Fleet-street, with their two heads as near to one another as the two eyes of each were, bore a considerable resemblance to a pair of monkeys. The resemblance was not lessened by the accidental circumstance, that the mature Jerry bit and spat out straw, while the twinkling eyes of the youthful Jerry were as restlessly watchful of him as of everything else in Fleet-street.

The head of one of the regular indoor messengers attached to Tellson's establishment was put through the door, and the word was given:

"Porter wanted!"

"Hooray, father! Here's an early job to begin with!"

A Tale of Two Cities is a story cast at the time of the French Revolution. The two cities are Paris and London. The central character, Alexandre Manette, is released from prison in Paris, where he has been held because, in his work as a doctor, he had found out compromising information about a powerful family. He relocates to

© The Author(s), under exclusive license to Springer Nature Switzerland AG 2023   11
G. Johnes, *Economics for Lovers of Literature*,
https://doi.org/10.1007/978-3-031-26486-3_3

London to join his daughter. The book is famous for its opening line: 'It was the best of times, it was the worst of times...'—people of different stations and in different places experience the same time differently. Espionage and murder are both upfront in the plot. Like much of Dickens' oeuvre, themes of social justice are to the fore, and the book served as a warning to those in power in England. I was reading this book the last time I visited Paris—a visit that I am unlikely to be allowed to forget because at the end of our stay, I took my family to the airport to make the journey home... only to find that I had taken them to Charles De Gaulle airport instead of Orly. Oops.

The taxi company employed by Walter Shandy would not be able to make substantial profits for long. New firms would probably see the opportunities offered by the taxi trade and would enter the industry, providing competition at cut prices.

In The Tale of Two Cities, Jeremiah Cruncher is (what we'll generously call) a 'small businessman' who likewise enters (what we'll generously describe as) an 'industry'. He carries things. In other words, he is a porter. His main role is as a porter for Tellson's Bank. Once something needs moving, or a message needs to be taken somewhere, he springs into action. And that is how he earns his pay. His costs are essentially zero—he just sits outside the bank waiting for the call to run an errand. His revenue comes from the payment he receives for running the errand. Hopefully his revenues give him enough to live on. (If they do not, he can always do some 'moonlighting'—Jeremiah has a sideline in another, less savoury, type of running and carrying; he digs up bodies from graveyards and sells them for use in the medical trades.) If he does particularly well in his day job, other people will see that it is lucrative. He will then face competition as more 'small businessmen' wait outside the bank's doors in the hope of receiving a call to run errands. These new entrants to the 'industry' will seek a foothold, making themselves attractive to Tellson's (and potentially other clients) by undercutting Jeremiah's price. Jeremiah will be forced to respond by himself reducing his price. The bank may decide that, at the more attractive prices, more errand-running tasks become worthwhile, so the lower prices may serve to raise demand for portering services. Either way, the surpluses earned by Jeremiah fall due to the new competition. Meanwhile the surpluses earned by the bank increase—both because they can now pay less per errand and because they can increase the number of errands undertaken. Competition among the porters may be bad news for the porters, but it is certainly good news for their client(s).

The portering industry is interesting because it costs Jeremiah (and his competitors) virtually nothing to enter. He needs a stool to sit on—and that's it. He does not need premises in which to do his work, he does not need to invest in expensive tools and machinery, and he does not need to recruit and train a workforce of skilled employees. All of this keeps his costs down (virtually to zero), but there is a downside—it becomes very easy indeed for competitors to enter his patch. For sure there are things that Jerry could do to make it harder for these competitors. He could negotiate terms with the bank—so, for example, he could agree with them that only uniformed workers could run errands for the bank. But that would raise his own costs as well as those of potential competitors. Or, with doubtful legality, he could threaten competitors with violence. But that cuts two ways and he may come off the worse for any fight. So it looks as though the 'industry' in which Jeremiah works is characterised by close to perfect competition.

The salient characteristics of such perfect competition are that there should be many buyers (in this case banks and other clients), many sellers (providers of services like Jeremiah), perfect information and perfect mobility (so that buyers can perceive and switch to the provider that offers the best value), and that the sellers should (as they do in the errand-running case) offer identical products. Taken together, these conditions ensure that buyers will gravitate towards the lowest price on offer. With all sellers trying to undercut one another's price, the price offered by each of them will gravitate towards the lowest possible price—that is, the price below which the supplier would make no profit at all. For Jeremiah, this would not be zero. Rather it would be the lowest price that keeps him engaged in his portering business. At some point, presumably, the price could fall below this, and he would switch out of portering altogether in order to concentrate on other activities—finding a job elsewhere, or maybe unearthing more corpses. Basically, this means that the price charged by all suppliers is driven down by the competition to the level of costs. Revenues equal costs, so the costs are covered—just—and no profit is earned.

The revenue earned by a firm is determined by the price that it charges and the quantity that it sells. As we have seen, in a highly competitive context, the price that the firm charges is competed down to the level of costs. It is interesting then to consider how the firm decides what quantity of its output it should produce and sell. In doing so, it is useful to begin by considering the technology that is used in the firm's production process. In Jeremiah's case, the technology is very simple, but nevertheless, it is worth considering exactly how, and at what cost, he converts the inputs into his production process into outputs.

Essentially, Jeremiah's output is his provision of messaging services, and his input is his time. Running one, and only one, errand in a day would be quite costly to him. He would need to travel from home to his station outside Tellson's Bank before he even begins to work—and of course at the end of the day he would need to travel back. If he walks, there is no financial cost, but he nonetheless has to sacrifice the time involved in the journey; if he uses public transport, he must also bear the financial cost of the fare. This is a fixed cost associated with his work for the day. If he runs two or more errands, he can spread this fixed cost over however many errands he undertakes, and so the cost of providing each errand falls as the number of errands increases. At some point, though, this cost is likely to rise, because Jeremiah would have so much work to do that he would have to hire an assistant to run some of the errands for him. So, as his firm's output increases there are reasons to suppose that the cost that Jeremiah incurs per errand go down, and other reasons to suppose that the cost rises. Competitive pressure should push Jeremiah to produce at the very lowest feasible level of cost per errand, and the number of errands that he supplies will be determined by the technology delivering that minimum cost.

More generally, businesses tend to experience economies of scale that ensure that, as their output grows, the cost of producing each unit of output falls. But this happens only up to a point. As firms get very large, these economies of scale get exhausted and the per unit cost of production bottoms out. It may even start rising as a result of diseconomies of scale if factors such as bureaucracy and coordination challenges offset the advantages of large size. Again, competition will drive firms to produce whatever amount of output leads to the cost per unit produced being minimised—and also to set their price at whatever the cost per unit produced might be at that point.

This has an important implication. Competition ensures that firms produce as efficiently as they possibly can. Of course, not all things are produced in an industrial setting that is as competitive as Jeremiah's errand-running business. So efficiency may not be something that we see around us all the time. But where competition is intense, we should expect to see production taking place efficiently. That is a good thing because it means that inputs are being converted into outputs with as little waste as possible. Indeed, it's such a good thing that we'll spend more time exploring the idea in greater depth later on.

In the meantime, though, let's run a mind experiment. If there are many firms in the industry and they all have access to the same technology, then the way that each firm's costs vary with its level of production should be similar to all the other firms. Each firm should be producing the same amount, incurring the same cost per unit of output, and charging the same price. (Inevitably firms aren't really exactly identical, but let's run with the ideas here and consider them to be at least approximately an accurate depiction of the reality.) Now suppose that demand for the product being produced in this industry increases—right across the board. (Maybe, in Jeremiah's industry, a big news story has just broken that leads to a huge increase in the number of communications that all banks must have with their customers.) The immediate effect of this increase in demand is to create a situation in which the current level of production, at current prices, does not meet the demand. Firms find that they can raise their price and still sell. So the prices charged by all firms in the industry go up. At this new price, though, firms are likely to be willing to increase their supply. Jeremiah may be willing to work a little overtime, or to hire an assistant. The amount the firms are willing to produce is still determined by their technology and the impact that that technology has on their costs, but, since the price commanded by the market has increased, so too (typically) does the amount that they can produce. To be specific, the firm will raise production to the point where the price received is just sufficient to cover the cost of producing the last unit of output produced. In a nutshell, firms' costs determine the amount that they are willing to supply to the market.

If the last unit produced by the firm costs more to produce than the price at which the firm can sell it, the firm will choose not to produce it. That is the essence of supply. And, as we saw earlier, if the utility that a consumer gets from consuming an extra unit of a good is lower than the price of the good, then he or she will choose not to consume it. That is the essence of demand. Market forces—the natural adjustments of price to a glut or a shortage—ensure that demand and supply cannot be out of balance with each other for long. In so doing, they ensure also that consumers are consuming up to the point where they cannot enjoy further gains by consuming more and that producers are producing up to the point where they cannot enjoy further gains by producing more. Where markets operate perfectly, they ensure the best possible economic outcome. We shall explore this further in the next chapter.

Think about someone you know who runs a small business—perhaps a personal fitness trainer, or a hairdresser. Where did they take their holiday last year? Why don't they raise their prices so that they can afford a better vacation?

Chapter 4
Economic Welfare—Why Trade Is Good: Part 1

From Mary Hallock Foote: The Desert and the Sown

I stayed out all that winter, workin' towards the coast. One day, along in March, I fetched a charcoal burner's camp, and the critter took me in and nursed my frost-bites and didn't ask no questions, nor I of him. We struck up a trade, my drivin' stock, mostly skin and bone, for a show in his business. He wa'n't gettin' rich at it, that was as plain as the hip bones on my mules. I kep' in the woods, cuttin' timber and tendin' kiln, and he hauled and did the sellin'. Next year he went below to Portland and brought home smallpox with him. It broke out on him on the road. He was a terrible sick man. I buried him, and waited for my turn. It didn't come. I seemed kind o' insured. I've been in lots of trouble since then, but nothing ever touched me till now. I banked on it too strong, though. I sure did! My pardner was just such another lone bird like me. If he had any folks of his own he kep' still about them. So I took his name—whether it was his name there's no knowing. Guess I've took full as good care of it as he would. 'Hagar?' folk would say, sort o' lookin' me over. 'You ain't Jim Hagar.' No, but I was John, and they let it go at that.

Mary Hallock Foote wrote stories about the American West around the turn of the twentieth century. In the Desert and the Sown, the focus is on physical separation within a family—though this theme extends to similar tensions, between the quest for liberty and stability, also at the level of society. To add some excitement the book involves an unlawful killing and even includes a ghost story. In the above extract, Adam Bogardus, who spent time travelling around the West away from his family, tells part of his story, showing how he earned his living. He and his business partner were struggling to make enough to stay in operation, and were clearly facing intense competition. Curiously, in real life, Adam Bogardus was the name of a champion shooter and inventor of a precursor of the type of trap used in clay pigeon shooting—he later joined Buffalo Bill's Wild West Show, and I have long wondered whether this Adam was the inspiration for Hallock Foote's fictional Adam.

© The Author(s), under exclusive license to Springer Nature Switzerland AG 2023   17
G. Johnes, *Economics for Lovers of Literature*,
https://doi.org/10.1007/978-3-031-26486-3_4

Manufacturing charcoal is a simple process that involves cutting wood and heating it in a kiln with limited oxygen so that it does not burn. In the American West of the nineteenth century, settlers had been attracted by the availability of land that was sold to them at very low prices, or even given to them, by the governing authorities who needed to promote settlement as a means of developing the areas under their jurisdiction. This made it cheap to enter an industry that involved forestry—whether for timber production or the production of charcoal. There were many providers in the industry, each owning sufficient land to provide the wood required to keep them in business. But the fact that there were so many providers meant that the price of the finished product was driven down till it was no more than the cost of production. In the peculiar context of the American frontier, forested land was a plentiful resource. Hence Jim Hagar and Adam Bogardus were not getting rich at it.

By driving down the price as far as it can go, perfect competition ensures that the demand for the product—in this case charcoal—is high. While no one firm in the industry is producing particularly large amounts of charcoal, the total amount produced by the industry as a whole (adding the output of all firms in the industry together) is considerable. So a lot is produced, and it is sold at as low a price as can possibly be achieved. The consumers of charcoal are benefitting in two ways—they are consuming a lot of charcoal, and they are doing so at an attractive price. The surplus that consumers gain by paying a lower price for a product than they are, in principle, willing to pay is as large as it can possibly get. Utility that is enjoyed over and above the price that people pay is maximised. This is a good thing. Good for the people that buy Jim and Adam's charcoal.

The downside, of course, is that it is not so good for Jim and Adam. Because competitive pressure pushes the price at which they can sell down to the level of the cost of production, they can make no profit. If, somehow, they could push the price up so that it was greater than the cost of production, they could earn some profit—that would be at the expense of the consumers (who would then have to pay more per unit of charcoal, and who would then choose to buy less charcoal because of the higher price). But in this situation, the gain to the producer would not be as great as the loss to the consumers. This is because the higher price enjoyed by the producer is associated with a lower level of sales than we see when the lower price is enjoyed by the consumers.

This has a huge implication. Conditions of perfect competition maximise economic welfare. Competition drives the price to a level that ensures that the surpluses that are realised by trade between buyers and sellers are as great as they possibly can be. This observation is often attributed to the great economist, Adam Smith, who coined the term 'invisible hand' to describe the process where apparently uncoordinated competition between many buyers and sellers leads to the best possible outcome. The idea predates Smith, though. In 1705, Bernard Mandeville published his poem, The Grumbling Hive: or Knaves Turn'd Honest, which, in an amusing way, presents a similar argument.

A spacious hive well stocked with bees,
that lived in luxury and ease;
and yet as famed for laws and arms
as yielding large and early swarms;
was counted the great nursery
of sciences and industry…
Vast numbers thronged the fruitful hive;
yet those vast numbers made them thrive;
millions endeavouring to supply
each other's lust and vanity…
Bare virtue can't make nations live
in splendour; they, that would revive
a golden age, must be as free,
for acorns, as for honesty.

The fable of the bees and Adam Smith's invisible hand are often used to make the case for a free market economy. Leaving the economy to its own devices, it is argued, leads to the best possible outcomes. Maybe, to an approximation, that is right; maybe it is not. While the magic of the invisible hand is certainly appealing, there are interesting and important circumstances in which it does not work. These are the subject of the next few chapters.

If leaving the economy to its own devices maximises welfare, consider under what circumstances *not* leaving it to its own devices might be appropriate.

Chapter 5
Monopoly—Last Copy, Sir: Double Price

From Mark Twain: The Innocents Abroad

But in Naples I think they speculate on misfortunes of that kind. Papers are suppressed there every day, and spring up the next day under a new name. During the ten days or a fortnight we staid there one paper was murdered and resurrected twice. The newsboys are smart there, just as they are elsewhere. They take advantage of popular weaknesses. When they find they are not likely to sell out, they approach a citizen mysteriously, and say in a low voice—"Last copy, sir: double price; paper just been suppressed!" The man buys it, of course, and finds nothing in it. They do say—I do not vouch for it—but they do say that men sometimes print a vast edition of a paper, with a ferociously seditious article in it, distribute it quickly among the newsboys, and clear out till the Government's indignation cools. It pays well.

Mark Twain is, of course, best known for books chronicling youth in the deep south—notably Tom Sawyer and Huckleberry Finn—with themes criticising social conservatism and racism. The Innocents Abroad is different in that it is not a novel, but a travel book, and it documents the author's journey around the Mediterranean in 1867. Early parts of the book are, to a modern reader, strikingly lacking in political correctness, but towards the end, Twain famously concludes that 'travel is fatal to prejudice, bigotry and narrow-mindedness'. The Innocents Abroad is clearly the work of a novelist—it is not a gazetteer, but rather it is constructed around themes concerning the relationship between culture and history. These themes echo those of Twain's more familiar fictional work. The suppression of news described by Twain may have been a characteristic of Naples—a city that had only become a part of the Kingdom of Italy earlier in the decade—but the behaviour of the newsboy described here resonates far more widely. This is a great book to read when you are on a Mediterranean cruise, though it may make you jealous when you read about places that your ship fails to visit.

The magic of perfect competition—the invisible hand that guides the economy to the best possible outcome—is dazzlingly brilliant. The seemingly chaotic behaviour

© The Author(s), under exclusive license to Springer Nature Switzerland AG 2023   21
G. Johnes, *Economics for Lovers of Literature*,
https://doi.org/10.1007/978-3-031-26486-3_5

of masses of uncoordinated consumers and a plethora of businesses, each acting in their own interest, results in an outcome for society that cannot be bettered. Little wonder that many have been seduced by the logic of the model.

If, however, it seems too good to be true, maybe that's because it is. Perfect competition requires there to be a large number of buyers and sellers in the market so that no one buyer or seller has the power to impose a price that is different from the price attached to other trades. Mark Twain's newsboy has found a way to circumvent his weakness in the market—he claims to be selling the last available copy of the newspaper (and, to add to the tease, suggests that there is something really worth reading in it). In other words, he presents himself as the only vendor from which the newspaper can be bought. He acquires the characteristics of a monopoly—the sole seller of a particular type of product.

A monopolist is very different from a firm operating under conditions of perfect competition. As the only provider in the market, the monopolist enjoys a lot of discretion. In particular, it does not face the downward pressure that competition exerts on the price at which it sells its product. This means that the monopolist can charge a price that is higher than the price that would be charged by firms operating under perfectly competitive conditions. That means that the monopolist's price can rise to a level that is above costs, so the monopolist can make a profit. This is obviously good news for the monopolist—the profit represents a surplus, a gain that the monopolist makes over and above what it needs to make in order to keep it in business. The monopolist will keep cutting its output, and so raising the price at which it can sell that output, so long as what it gains from the increased price is at least as much as what it loses from the reduction in sales volume. Put another way, the monopolist will produce up to the point where selling one more unit adds just as much to costs as it does to revenues.

All of this is not such good news for consumers, who must pay more. Moreover, in selling only to those willing to pay the higher price, the monopolist chooses to exclude some prospective customers from access to the product. The higher price means that there is less demand, and so less is sold and less is produced. It is characteristic of monopolistic provision that the price is higher, and the quantity is lower than is the case under perfect competition.

The separation between price and cost has a further important implication. Some prospective customers would be willing to pay a price that (while being lower than the price the monopolist chooses to charge) is higher than the amount it costs the firm to produce the product, but the firm nonetheless refuses to sell to them. At first sight, this seems surprising—even though the firm could increase its profit by selling to these people, it decides not to. The reason is that, if it were to allow some customers to undercut its posted price, it would undermine its own pricing decisions—and it would then have to reduce the price it charged to everyone else. In effect, the firm refuses to sell to some potential customers because it needs to do this to bolster the price it can receive from other customers.

Consequently some trades that—in the sense that they would benefit both parties—ought to happen don't happen when there is a monopoly. This means that monopoly leads to inefficiency. It would, in principle, be possible to make both the frustrated buyer and the monopolist better off (if only they could settle on a price that did not compromise the monopolist's ability to charge high prices to other customers). Furthermore, since the monopolist produces at a level of output that differs from that chosen by firms facing perfect competition, monopolies do not minimise unit costs. In short, the magic of perfect competition is absent from a monopoly.

In one respect there is nothing surprising about this. Nobody enjoys the sensation of being exploited. Monopolists use their market power to exploit their customers. If there is nowhere else the customer can go for the product, they must either buy from the monopolist (at a price above cost) or go without. But it is important to emphasise that the inefficiency of a monopoly is about more than customers feeling ripped off. While monopoly power makes buyers worse off, it also makes the seller better off—the monopolist earns a profit. The key insight, however, is that, because of the monopolist's inefficiency—because trades that ought to happen don't happen—the gain to the producer does not fully offset the losses to the consumers. Monopoly power erodes the overall value of the surpluses that are made through trade.

Since monopolists make profits, one might expect other firms, attracted by the prospect of making profits themselves, to try to enter the industry. If they were to succeed, the monopoly would be short-lived, and competitive pressures would lower the price over time and thereby restore efficiency. Often, though, monopolists can defend their dominant position in the market. They may have privileged access to something that is needed for the production of the product. De Beers is a company that has bought a considerable proportion of the world's land used for diamond mining, and so it has monopoly power in the diamond industry. In other firms, the source of monopoly is know-how: KFC jealously protects its secret recipe of spices with which it coats its fried chicken. Twain's newsboy creates a myth—that he is the last source standing for today's newspaper, and no more copies will be printed.

In some industries, delivery of the product involves the creation of a network. Landline telephone, internet, and cable TV services, the distribution of water, gas and electricity and a country's network of railway tracks provide examples. In these cases, once a network has been set up, a firm owning the network can operate as a monopoly and can know that prospective competitors would have to invest in creating a whole second network. This would be an expensive and wasteful undertaking. The existence of a single network allows the firm that owns that network to expand delivery of the product while reducing unit costs (since the cost of setting up the network is spread over more units of output). So expanding the sole provider is less costly than setting up a second provider. This situation of natural monopoly is one where there are certainly benefits to having just one provider—but those benefits need to be balanced against the costs of giving one firm such a lot of market power.

Other contexts exist where the service being provided by a firm is essentially one of bringing people together. The internet auction site, eBay, brings together buyers and sellers. If you want to sell something, you choose to use a site that many buyers visit. Likewise, if you want to buy something, you maximise your chances of finding it by visiting a site that many sellers use. It would therefore be difficult for a new firm to compete with eBay, simply because it would be hard for it to acquire the critical mass of activity quickly enough. Many apps used in the gig economy bring service users and service providers together in exactly this way—think of Uber (providing cab rides), or MTurk (providing all sorts of micro jobs). The cost of entering these industries may be quite low, so competitors (such as Lyft in the market for rides) may emerge from time to time, but the benefits of bringing as many buyers as possible into contact with as many sellers as possible will make it highly likely that a process of mergers and takeovers will leave industries of this type with a single dominant firm.

Another barrier that makes entry into an industry difficult is the brand identity of existing providers. Where incumbent firms have a strong brand, it can be difficult and costly for new competitors to gain a foothold, simply because existing firms enjoy the benefits of customer recognition. This source of monopoly power is very important because it is one that can easily be manipulated by the existing providers. Even where the product being provided is difficult to distinguish from the products that competitors could provide, branding can change consumers' perceptions and lead to them having strong preferences that, in effect, give the supplier some measure of monopoly power. One can of baked beans may be much like another, but people tend to have their preferred brands, and successful brands can charge a premium. Even if you are selling reams of blank A4 paper, having a brand can help you distinguish your product from the competition, charge a premium, and make a profit.

For all of these reasons, firms can achieve at least some degree of monopoly power, restrict their sales in order to raise the price and drive a wedge between that price and the cost of production. That wedge is what they need to make a profit, but it is also what leads to the inefficient situation where trades that could benefit both buyer and seller are not made (because the seller is unwilling to undermine the price at which it sells to everyone else).

The attempts made by firms to gain market power—through, for example, advertising and branding—are, arguably at least, another source of inefficiency that is widely observed where competition is not perfect. Various statistical exercises have been conducted that quantify the total inefficiency due to monopoly power (as a total for advertising, branding, other 'rent seeking' activity, producing at higher cost than necessary, and failing to complete desirable trades) at between 10 and 15% of the value of all economic activity in the economy.[1]

The proneness of monopolies to inefficiency has led governments to try to regulate them in order to curb their worst excesses. Regulations can take a number of forms, including price caps (often seen in the energy industries). In some cases, such as the food retail sector, regulation can even take the form of companies being forced to sell some of their outlets to competitors.

It is worth noting an important exception to the general rule that monopolies are inefficient. Some monopolies produce bespoke products and can charge a different price to each customer. Indeed they might be able to charge each customer the most that the customer is willing to pay. In such circumstances, the firm would find it worthwhile to produce and sell to every customer that is able to at least meet the costs

---

[1] Many relevant studies are cited in a survey by Ignacio del Rosal (2011) The empirical measurement of rent seeking costs, *Journal of Economic Surveys*, 25, 298–325.

of production. So the output level would be the same as in the perfectly competitive case and there would be no inefficiency—but all the surplus would go to the firm and none to the consumer. Pure price discrimination of this kind is highly unusual, but there are plenty of examples where firms do discriminate between groups of customers—think, for example, of discounted train tickets for people who can travel at off-peak times, happy hours in pubs, or student discounts at restaurants. These all exist to raise the profit of the firm, but in so doing they alleviate some of the economic inefficiency of the monopoly.

Mark Twain's newsboy has robbed the gleaming image of the competitive firm of some of its lustre. He presents as a somewhat tawdry spiv, perhaps being economical with the truth in order to gain a sale at an inflated price, exploiting the poor punter as he does so. Caricatures aside, monopoly does, as we have seen, reduce economic welfare by blocking trades that, in an efficient world, should take place. That firms can, at least to some extent, create their own monopoly power through developing a strong brand suggests that the magical world of perfect competition might not be the place to which a free market gravitates. Now whether you see yourself surrounded by the purity of perfect competition or rather by the dirt of monopoly depends in large part on whether you are a glass half full or glass half empty kind of person. There are good reasons to think that leaving the economy to do its own thing results in the best possible outcomes. But there are also good reasons to think that the economy needs a helping hand.

Both perfect competition and monopoly are extreme cases. Most industries are somewhere in between, and are comprised of a small number of firms (or possibly a small number of large, dominant firms alongside a competitive fringe of smaller providers). The case of industries with a small number of major players is particularly interesting—each firm has some market power and produces less efficiently than a perfectly competitive firm but more efficiently than a monopoly. Their market power means that they can influence the environment faced by other firms, while at the same time they are themselves influenced by what other firms do. In effect, these firms are playing games of strategy with each other, and this will be the subject of our next chapter.

To what extent do you consider the advent of digital technologies has increased or decreased the monopoly power of businesses in various industries?

Chapter 6
Oligopoly and Game Theory—The Kursaal Flyers

From Jonathan Swift: A Tale of a Tub

They both unanimously entered upon this great work, looking sometimes on their coats and sometimes on the will. Martin laid the first hand; at one twitch brought off a large handful of points, and with a second pull stripped away ten dozen yards of fringe. But when he had gone thus far he demurred a while. He knew very well there yet remained a great deal more to be done; however, the first heat being over, his violence began to cool, and he resolved to proceed more moderately in the rest of the work, having already very narrowly escaped a swinging rent in pulling off the points, which being tagged with silver (as we have observed before), the judicious workman had with much sagacity double sewn to preserve them from falling. Resolving therefore to rid his coat of a huge quantity of gold lace, he picked up the stitches with much caution and diligently gleaned out all the loose threads as he went, which proved to be a work of time. Then he fell about the embroidered Indian figures of men, women, and children, against which, as you have heard in its due place, their father's testament was extremely exact and severe. These, with much dexterity and application, were after a while quite eradicated or utterly defaced. For the rest, where he observed the embroidery to be worked so close as not to be got away without damaging the cloth, or where it served to hide or strengthen any flaw in the body of the coat, contracted by the perpetual tampering of workmen upon it, he concluded the wisest course was to let it remain, resolving in no case whatsoever that the substance of the stuff should suffer injury, which he thought the best method for serving the true intent and meaning of his father's will. And this is the nearest account I have been able to collect of Martin's proceedings upon this great revolution.

But his brother Jack, whose adventures will be so extraordinary as to furnish a great part in the remainder of this discourse, entered upon the matter with other thoughts and a quite different spirit. For the memory of Lord Peter's injuries produced a degree of hatred and spite which had a much greater share of

G. Johnes, *Economics for Lovers of Literature*,
https://doi.org/10.1007/978-3-031-26486-3_6

inciting him than any regards after his father's commands, since these appeared at best only secondary and subservient to the other. However, for this medley of humour he made a shift to find a very plausible name, honouring it with the title of zeal, which is, perhaps, the most significant word that has been ever yet produced in any language, as, I think, I have fully proved in my excellent analytical discourse upon that subject, wherein I have deduced a histori-theo-physiological account of zeal, showing how it first proceeded from a notion into a word, and from thence in a hot summer ripened into a tangible substance. This work, containing three large volumes in folio, I design very shortly to publish by the modern way of subscription, not doubting but the nobility and gentry of the land will give me all possible encouragement, having already had such a taste of what I am able to perform.

I record, therefore, that brother Jack, brimful of this miraculous compound, reflecting with indignation upon Peter's tyranny, and further provoked by the despondency of Martin, prefaced his resolutions to this purpose. "What!" said he, "a rogue that locked up his drink, turned away our wives, cheated us of our fortunes, palmed his crusts upon us for mutton, and at last kicked us out of doors; must we be in his fashions? A rascal, besides, that all the street cries out against." Having thus kindled and inflamed himself as high as possible, and by consequence in a delicate temper for beginning a reformation, he set about the work immediately, and in three minutes made more dispatch than Martin had done in as many hours. For, courteous reader, you are given to understand that zeal is never so highly obliged as when you set it a-tearing; and Jack, who doted on that quality in himself, allowed it at this time its full swing. Thus it happened that, stripping down a parcel of gold lace a little too hastily, he rent the main body of his coat from top to bottom; and whereas his talent was not of the happiest in taking up a stitch, he knew no better way than to darn it again with packthread thread and a skewer. But the matter was yet infinitely worse (I record it with tears) when he proceeded to the embroidery; for being clumsy of nature, and of temper impatient withal, beholding millions of stitches that required the nicest hand and sedatest constitution to extricate, in a great rage he tore off the whole piece, cloth and all, and flung it into the kennel, and furiously thus continuing his career, "Ah! good brother Martin," said he, "do as I do, for the love of God; strip, tear, pull, rend, flay off all that we may appear as unlike that rogue Peter as it is possible. I would not for a hundred pounds carry the least mark about me that might give occasion to the neighbours of suspecting I was related to such a rascal." But Martin, who at this time happened to be extremely phlegmatic and sedate, begged his brother, of all love, not to damage his coat by any means, for he never would get such another; desired him to consider that it was not their business to form their actions by any reflection upon Peter's, but by observing the rules prescribed in their father's will. That he should remember Peter was still their brother, whatever faults or injuries he had committed, and therefore they should by all means avoid such a thought as that of taking measures for good and evil from no other rule than of opposition to him. That it was true the testament of their good father was very exact in what related to the wearing of their coats; yet was it no less penal and strict in prescribing agreement, and friendship, and affection between them. And therefore, if straining a point were at all defensible, it would certainly be so rather to the advance of unity than increase of contradiction.

Martin had still proceeded as gravely as he began, and doubtless would have delivered an admirable lecture of morality, which might have exceedingly contributed to my reader's repose both of body and mind (the true ultimate end of ethics), but Jack was already gone a flight-shot beyond his patience. And as in scholastic disputes nothing serves to rouse the spleen of him that opposes so much as a kind of pedantic affected calmness in the respondent, disputants being for the most part like unequal scales, where the gravity of one side advances the lightness of the other, and causes it to fly up and kick the beam; so it happened here that the weight of Martin's arguments exalted Jack's levity, and made him fly out and spurn against his brother's moderation. In short, Martin's patience put Jack in a rage; but that which most afflicted him was to observe his brother's coat so well reduced into the state of innocence, while his own was either wholly rent to his shirt, or those places which had escaped his cruel clutches were still in Peter's livery. So that he looked like a drunken beau half rifled by bullies, or like a fresh tenant of Newgate when he has refused the payment of garnish, or like a discovered shoplifter left to the mercy of Exchange-women, or like a bawd in her old velvet petticoat resigned into the secular hands of the mobile. Like any or like all of these, a medley of rags, and lace, and fringes, unfortunate Jack did now appear; he would have been extremely glad to see his coat in the condition of Martin's, but infinitely gladder to find that of Martin in the same predicament with his. However, since neither of these was likely to come to pass, he thought fit to lend the whole business another turn, and to dress up necessity into a virtue. Therefore, after as many of the fox's arguments as he could muster up for bringing Martin to reason, as he called it, or as he meant it, into his own ragged, bobtailed condition, and observing he said all to little purpose, what alas! was left for the forlorn Jack to do, but, after a million of scurrilities against his brother, to run mad with spleen, and spite, and contradiction. To be short, here began a mortal breach between these two. Jack went immediately to new lodgings, and in a few days it was for certain reported that he had run out of his wits. In a short time after he appeared abroad, and confirmed the report by falling into the oddest whimsies that ever a sick brain conceived.

A century and a half before Lawrence Sterne introduced Tristram Shandy's digressions to the world, there was Jonathan Swift and A Tale of A Tub. On the surface, it's a story of three brothers. But each brother represents a branch of Christianity— Roman Catholic (Peter), Anglican (Jack), and dissenting protestant (Martin)—and the whole story is a satire on these established religions. In particular, it focuses on how each denomination makes changes in response to actions of the others— symbolised by changes made by each brother to his own coat. The behaviour of the religious groups at the time was closely wrapped up with politics—the book was written soon after the Glorious Revolution in which the Catholic King James II had been deposed in favour of the Protestant William of Orange, abandoning the principle of absolute monarchy in favour of parliamentary democracy. Political strategy at the time, just as now, had much in common with games of strategy such as chess. More recently, another great piece of literature points to the importance of getting into the other players' minds when playing a game of strategy—one-hit wonders, the Kursaal Flyers, had a song which went 'Little does she know that I know that she knows that I know she's cheating on me...'. That song ear-worms me every time I think about competition between a small number of firms.

Firms in perfectly competitive industries must produce at the lowest possible unit cost in order to survive. They only need to examine their own data on costs in order to know what they must do—how much they should produce and what price they should charge. Monopolies likewise only have to examine their own data; they have no competitors. The first Delphic maxim—'know thyself'—makes a fine rule for firms to follow in both these extreme forms of market structure.

It's a fine place to start in other (and more common) industrial settings too. But where there are several competitors, each with some degree of power in the market, it is far from sufficient for a firm just to know itself. It must know all the other firms too. This is because, just as is the case with Swift's Martin and Jack, what one firm does matters to the other—and what the other does matters to the first.

Martin and Jack bring to mind a story about two people taking a walk in a wood. They see a bear and both run to try to escape. As they run, one of them laments the fact that the bear is too fast and there is no point in running away. The other replies 'But I don't have to run faster than the bear—I only have to run faster than you'.

The brothers in Swift's story vie with one another by adorning their coats. If one brother ups the ante, the others must respond. Firms operating in an environment where each of them has some degree of market power must similarly respond to each other's actions. More than this, they must recognise that their own actions will trigger some sort of response on the part of their competitors.

Competition between firms, each of whom has market power, can take a number of forms. The firms could compete on price, or they could compete on advertising, or they could compete on the quantity of output produced. The advertising war between Pepsi and Coca-Cola is particularly notable. Pepsi has used celebrities such as Michael Jackson, Beyonce and Shakira in their advertising, while Coca-Cola have used Elton John, will.i.am and Selena Gomez; Pepsi has a sponsorship deal with the NFL, while Coca-Cola has a deal with the Olympics.

Competition on the basis of the quantity produced is particularly interesting. If companies in the industry are producing identical (or almost identical) products, then, other things being equal, an increase in supply by just one company has an impact on all the other companies in the industry because it forces down the price at which the output of the industry can be sold. This means that each company must make its decisions in an uncertain environment; no company knows how much other companies will choose to produce, and so each company faces uncertainty about the price at which it will be able to sell its output.

This uncertainty may, at first blush, appear very daunting. It certainly introduces more complexity to the decision-making of a firm than is apparent in simpler types of market. Yet it turns out that firms can determine their best strategy to adopt even in the face of such uncertainty.

Recall that a monopolist chooses to produce up to the point where producing one more unit would add just as much to costs as it does to revenues. The same principle holds good for any other firm that wants to make as much profit as possible. The difficulty, where there are a few powerful firms in the industry, is that each firm must decide how much to produce without knowing how much its competitors will produce—and so, crucially, also without knowing what price it will be able to sell its output for. That means that the firm does not know what revenue it can expect to earn from producing and selling any particular amount of output (though it does know how much it costs to produce that amount). Or so it seems.

However, it turns out that the first Delphic maxim can once again help. 'Know thyself' might be taken to mean that a firm should not only have data about its own costs and revenues. It should also have an understanding of what makes it tick—what its motivations are. And, crucially, through that introspection it should also have an understanding about what makes its competitors tick. If the firm that we are interested in seeks to earn as high a level of profit as possible, then it is likely that other firms are seeking the same thing for themselves. This gives our firm a key insight into the likely behaviour of other firms in the industry—and it tells us that those other firms have the same key insight into how our firm will behave too. So the process of making decisions in a market comprising a few powerful firms is one of figuring out what to do when we know that our choices have an impact on our competitors' environment and so also on their choices, and we understand also that those choices shape the context for our firm too. The reassuring thing is that our firm's competitors also have to make these calculations using a similar rationale. While we do not know for sure what they will choose, we do know that they will act in their own best interests (as they know we will act in ours), and this lends their actions some predictability. Our firm's strategy needs to take their firms' reactions into account, but these reactions are circumscribed by what works best for them. If we take as given that other firms will act in their own best interest (and if those other firms make a symmetric assumption about how we will behave), then on that basis our firm can calculate the level of output that maximises our profit—and every other firm in the industry can do so too. In this solution, no firm can unilaterally improve upon its position, so it seems to be a reasonable position at which an industry characterised by a few powerful firms would settle.

This point generally involves firms in the industry producing more than a monopolist would produce, and charging a lower price. Otherwise, there would be gain to the separate firms from colluding with each other and behaving as if they were a monopolist. However, the solution also involves firms in producing less than would be produced in a perfectly competitive industry, and in charging a higher price. The profit that each firm makes is obtained by setting the price above the lowest possible unit cost. So the solution for a market with a few powerful firms is somewhere between the extreme cases of perfect competition and monopoly. Since firms do drive a wedge between the price at which they are willing to sell, on the one hand, and the cost of production, on the other, and since they do not produce at the scale of output that would minimise unit cost, they do produce inefficiently and may therefore be subject to regulation.

The strategic problem described here is similar to that seen in many games. In chess, one player's move depends on the anticipated response of the other player (which is itself conditioned on the first player's past and expected future moves). In football, any decision to pass the ball forwards or backwards, left or right, is both influenced by and influences the movements of the other team's players. All of these examples of strategic interdependence have been analysed by game theory. The position at which the industry described above will settle is often described as a 'Cournot-Nash equilibrium' in honour of two of the intellectual giants of this field.[1]

The idea that no firm can unilaterally improve its position is important in the above description of how markets with several powerful players operate. Usually independent firms should be expected to behave unilaterally, but in some circumstances it might be profitable for them to work together. If the separate businesses can cooperate so that, in effect, they act like a monopolist, they can raise the price (by restricting output) and so increase their profit. Collusion of this type is illegal in many jurisdictions because it is designed specifically to undermine competition and reduce consumer welfare. The best examples of such behaviour are therefore international cartels, such as the OPEC oil cartel, that operate across the borders of many countries. Even in these cases, though, collusion is often short-lived. This is because, while cooperating (to raise the price by limiting output) is in the interest of all players, each player has a strong incentive to cheat by selling more output than they have agreed to sell. Once players cheat, the excess supply in the market drives the price down. With all players cheating, the market is likely to return to an uncooperative ('Cournot-Nash equilibrium') position.

Markets of this kind, with a few powerful players, are clearly quite complex. The strategic 'games' played by the players in the industry are sophisticated, but it is not difficult to see evidence of this type of strategic thinking in the behaviour of many firms. It just involves taking the 'know thyself' maxim a step further—firms need to understand their own position and that of their competitors, and they need to act in a way that takes their competitors' response into account. This might entail figuring out how best to act many moves into the future, at each move figuring out how to respond to each possible response by the opponent. Inevitably, in practice, given the complexity, mistakes are sometimes made; even in the absence of mistakes, decision-making in this type of market is, in practice, difficult.

The fundamental principle is quite easy though. Less so than a monopoly, but nevertheless to what might be a significant extent, markets where a few powerful firms exist impose a cost in terms of economic inefficiency. Peter, Jack and Martin might each have secured a better coat if they had not devoted so much energy to a strategic competition against one another.

Consider an industry where there are a few large firms—examples might be found in the energy industry, telecommunications, streaming services for

---

[1] A.A. Cournot (1838) Recherches sur les principes mathématiques de la théorie de la richesses, Paris: Vrin; J.F. Nash (1951) Non-cooperative games, Annals of Mathematics, 54, 286–295.

TV, supermarkets for groceries, or in a wide variety of other contexts. In what respects does a firm in the industry that you have chosen need to take into account strategic decisions made by its competitors?

Chapter 7
The Market for Labour—Gizza Job

From Charlotte Bronte: Shirley

At this crisis certain inventions in machinery were introduced into the staple manufactures of the north, which, greatly reducing the number of hands necessary to be employed, threw thousands out of work, and left them without legitimate means of sustaining life. A bad harvest supervened. Distress reached its climax. Endurance, overgoaded, stretched the hand of fraternity to sedition. The throes of a sort of moral earthquake were felt heaving under the hills of the northern counties. But, as is usual in such cases, nobody took much notice. When a food-riot broke out in a manufacturing town, when a gig-mill was burnt to the ground, or a manufacturer's house was attacked, the furniture thrown into the streets, and the family forced to flee for their lives, some local measures were or were not taken by the local magistracy. A ringleader was detected, or more frequently suffered to elude detection; newspaper paragraphs were written on the subject, and there the thing stopped. As to the sufferers, whose sole inheritance was labour, and who had lost that inheritance—who could not get work, and consequently could not get wages, and consequently could not get bread—they were left to suffer on, perhaps inevitably left. It would not do to stop the progress of invention, to damage science by discouraging its improvements; the war could not be terminated; efficient relief could not be raised. There was no help then; so the unemployed underwent their destiny—ate the bread and drank the waters of affliction.

Of the three Bronte sisters, Charlotte lived the longest. Yet she died at the age of only 38. She is best known as the author of Jane Eyre. But her later novel, Shirley, is packed with interest for an economist. It is, on the surface, a love contest between two friends—the relatively poor Caroline Helstone and the wealthy Shirley Keeldar—for the attention of millowner Robert Moore. But it is set at a time of industrial unrest, and the sympathies of the two women for the impoverished textile workers tear Robert in two directions. A shooting adds spice to the plot. Interestingly, Shirley had up to this time been a man's name—and the central character (whose parents had expected

© The Author(s), under exclusive license to Springer Nature Switzerland AG 2023
G. Johnes, *Economics for Lovers of Literature*,
https://doi.org/10.1007/978-3-031-26486-3_7

the birth of a boy and not prepared themselves for naming a girl) displays some masculine toughness. Caroline and Shirley are, respectively, Robert's yin and yang. I read this book quite recently, after moving to the area in which it is set. While there has been a lot of construction since Shirley was written, you can still see many of the buildings that feature in the book and it is easy to imagine how the area once looked.

During the eighteenth century, Britain industrialised rapidly. The textile industry in particular expanded, partly as the result of the triangular routes sailed by ships across the Atlantic, taking goods from Britain to Africa, slaves from Africa to America, and cotton from America to Britain. Further expansion and urbanisation followed the invention of the spinning jenny and flying shuttle during the middle part of that century. Prosperity was thus built on foundations both of inventiveness and exploitation. By the end of the century, however, tensions were starting to rise. The Napoleonic Wars had severe economic consequences, in terms both of the increase in taxation required to finance the military effort and the disruption of trade patterns. Further innovations in the latter part of the century, notably the spinning mule and the power loom, were seen by workers as a challenge.

A movement protesting against the impact of technology on workers gained ground during the decade of the 1810s. The protesters were known as Luddites, after a character known as Ned Ludd (who may be mythical, but may be based on Edward Ludlam from Anstey in Leicestershire[1]). Several decades earlier, in 1779, Ned had destroyed some mill machinery. The Luddites followed suit. Bronte's novel, Shirley, is set against this backdrop.

A key issue to consider here is the extent to which machinery is a substitute for labour, and the extent to which it complements labour. Machines need people to operate them but are often invented specifically in order to make easier some of the tasks that people previously performed themselves. So it is clear that people and machines are neither perfect substitutes for one another nor perfect complements. Introducing new technology can therefore result in workers becoming less valuable to their employers, but it is equally possible that it can make workers more valuable.

The idea that workers have value offers a clue about how the role played by labour should be analysed. Just as is the case for any other good or service, the market for labour comprises a demand side and a supply side. The supply of labour reflects people's willingness to work at various levels of the wage. If a firm offers a very low wage, it is unlikely to attract workers. People in search of work will eschew the opportunity to work for such a firm and will instead go to work for a competitor that offers a higher reward. As the wage offered by the firm rises, the supply of labour will (normally) rise as people find it more worthwhile to work there.

But how can the firm afford to increase its wage in this way? To understand this, it's first necessary to understand that firms do not demand labour for its own sake. (Neither do they demand any other factors of production, such as land or machinery, for their own sake.) Robert Moore, the mill owner in Bronte's book, would not have employed any workers if it were not for the fact that the workers produced things that Moore could then sell. He demanded labour because of the cloth that the labour

---

[1] An Edward Ludlam, son of William and Mary, was indeed born in Anstey in 1736.

produced (that is, because the labour was needed to convert raw cotton or wool into textiles), and because he could sell that cloth. Labour has value because the cloth has value. Moore knew that he had to pay his workers (because otherwise they would go and work elsewhere), but the absolute maximum that he would be prepared to pay each worker would be the amount that worker added to the value of his output of cloth. In a perfect labour market, workers would be able to move between employers easily so that wages are bid up to the value implied by their productivity.

This observation has several implications. First, workers who have different levels of productivity can earn different wages. Someone who, by virtue of having special skills or being educated to a high level, is highly productive can earn a higher wage than someone lacking those attributes. At a societal level, increasing the skills of a population can help increase the prosperity of the nation. Secondly, if productivity falls for some reason, then wages will fall too. In the 1810s, British textile firms found it difficult to sell their cloth on international markets. The Continental Blockade instigated by Napoleon had cut off British exports to Europe, and, while less successful, Jefferson's embargo made trade with the US more difficult as well. This meant that producers had to cut the price of the cloth they had produced in order to sell it at all. Yarn prices fell by about a third (even after allowing for inflation[2]) between the start and end of the decade. Consequently, the monetary value of the output of the typical worker fell, and so wages fell as well.

The relationship between workers and machines now becomes a key point of interest. Unlike workers—who are hired and so paid a wage per hour (or another unit of time) that they work—machines are bought.[3] Machines are expensive, but they typically operate for several, if not many, years. Businesses must therefore balance the costs of buying a machine against the stream of benefits that come from the operation of that machine over a long time into the future. If labour is paid low wages, the benefits of mechanisation are not very high, because labour can do the work cheaply. But as labour becomes more expensive, mechanisation becomes more appealing. In the 1810s, with the collapse of the market for textiles, wages started to look high relative to the productivity of the workforce. This, in itself, is likely to have been a trigger for increased mechanisation.

The phrase 'in a perfect labour market' appeared a little while ago. That phrase does a lot of heavy lifting. To be sure, the idea of a perfect labour market helps us understand the link between productivity and the demand for labour—and hence between productivity and the wage. In a basic sense, we can only afford to pay ourselves the value of what we produce. But in truth, the labour market is not comparable to the market for cut flowers or strawberries. Workers do not (normally) wake

---

[2] Inflation is discussed further in Chapter 15.

[3] Where, rather than being hired from the worker himself or herself, labour is bought, it constitutes slavery. Slavery is widely deemed to be unethical, and is illegal in many (but by no means all) countries. Moreover, it contributed historically to the development of many countries where it is now illegal. Slave owners dehumanise labour, treating it as an investment in capital—just another type of machine. Economic tools can be used to analyse slavery, but certain aspects of the labour market are absent—for instance, the willingness to supply effort in return for a wage is replaced by coercion.

up each morning and decide who they should sell their services to that particular day. More typically, they enter a contract with an employer and remain in employment with that employer for a long time. This gives the employer some leverage over the employee. Within limits, an employer may pay its employees less than the value that they add to the firm through their productivity—since the employer knows that workers are not constantly on the lookout for alternative employment. As a result, workers that move a lot between firms are able to ratchet up their pay, while those who do not tend to find their pay is relatively stagnant. (I wish somebody had told me that when I was younger!) This tendency for workers to stay with their employers for a long time is due to the fact that it is costly to search for alternative employment—it takes time, and it often takes financial resources too (including the cost of interview haircuts, clothes and travel).

Inertia on the part of workers means that the labour market is not 'perfect' in the sense of being a spot market. Wages do not adjust to bring demand and supply into line with each other at every point in time. At some times, wages may be above this level; relative to the case where demand and supply are equal, employers' surplus would then be lower, and, while the surplus gained by those in employment is greater, there would be fewer workers employed. Unemployment is thus an example of market failure, analogous to the situation in which monopoly providers of goods cause a loss of efficiency. The labour market is characterised by a number of institutions that create inertia—contracts, unions, even the concept of a 'job' (as a package made up of numerous tasks that could in principle each be delivered separately). So, perhaps more than any other part of the economy, the labour market is challenging the idea that a free market exists and operates well.

Nevertheless long-term relationships between workers and their employers offer benefits. Employers who believe their workers are likely to stay with the firm over a long period into the future are likely to invest resources in training those workers, and this enhances their productivity. They are likely also to develop a hierarchy so that workers who are particularly meritorious can be promoted within the firm. This provides workers at all levels with strong incentives to work hard and to be productive. The benefit of this long-term relationship is often described as 'good work'—stable employment with development opportunities and a career ladder. It may be contrasted with other types of employment, such as those found in the 'gig economy' where the relationship between employee and employer is a much shorter term (often as short as a few minutes), and where the incentives to enhance productivity over time are largely absent.

The inertia of employees offers employers a degree of market power. But another source of imperfection in the labour market is observed when workers fail to respond to market signals. If there is an excess supply of labour, the price of labour (that is, the wage) should fall. In the 1810s, workers were understandably reluctant to suffer repeated cuts in their pay, and found ways of resisting such cuts. If payment does not fall (enough) when the demand for labour falls, there will be an excess supply of labour—there will not be enough jobs to satisfy all those who want to work at the going wage. Under these circumstances, there is the potential for many people to lose their employment. In the 1810s, with no system of social security in place, this often meant that people had to enlist in the army or emigrate in search of alternative employment. In Bronte's fiction, however, altruistic philanthropists came to the rescue:

From Charlotte Bronte: Shirley

The fund prospered ... and this being judiciously managed, served for the present greatly to alleviate the distress of the unemployed poor. The neighbourhood seemed to grow calmer.

From George Eliot: The Mill on the Floss

"What I want, you know," said Mr Tulliver,—"what I want is to give Tom a good eddication; an eddication as'll be a bread to him. That was what I was thinking of when I gave notice for him to leave the academy at Lady-day. I mean to put him to a downright good school at Midsummer. The two years at th' academy'ud ha' done well enough, if I'd meant to make a miller and farmer of him, for he's had a fine sight more schoolin' nor *I* ever got. All the learnin' *my* father ever paid for was a bit o' birch at one end and the alphabet at th' other. But I should like Tom to be a bit of a scholard, so as he might be up to the tricks o' these fellows as talk fine and write with a flourish. It'ud be a help to me wi' these lawsuits, and arbitrations, and things.

The Mill on the Floss is a remarkable book about which I shall comment more in a later chapter. In the above extract, Jeremy Tulliver extols the value—and that's a keyword—of schooling.

Mr. Tulliver clearly took the view that education would equip his son, Tom, well in the labour force. In particular, it would teach him 'tricks', or, in other words, augment his skills. More highly skilled workers are likely to be more productive than others— because of their greater know-how, they can produce more (or more valuable) output in a given amount of time. Consequently, they can be paid a higher wage. Indeed, if they were not paid a higher wage in their current job, an alternative employer would likely try to attract them by offering better remuneration. Competition between employers would thus ensure that each worker is paid according to their contribution to the firm.

So education is an investment. Prolonging one's schooling involves an immediate sacrifice of earnings, but this is done in the belief that the skills acquired through education will enhance future earnings. In deciding whether or not to extend Tom's schooling, Mr Tulliver weighs up the costs against the benefits. These costs and benefits differ across people, and so some people choose to invest more in education than do others—and for the same reason there are differences in the specialisation chosen by different people. This is good because any society needs a population with a variety of skills.

From Bankim Chandra Chatterjee—Rajmohan's Wife

One good result however followed Ramkanai's residence in the metropolis. Influenced by the example of the metropolitans, he had bestowed on his son Madhav as good an education as he could receive in Calcutta... The father of Madhav died a little before the latter completed his studies at college... Madhav continued his studies till he finished them, his agents managing his estate for him during his absence and minority.

In Chatterjee's gripping page-turner, Rajmohan's young wife, Matangini, hears her husband plotting with others against Madhav (her sister's husband). A tangled love story spiced with intrigue and a string of kidnappings, attempted rapes and murders ensues. Madhav, whose education (and some lucky breaks) brought prosperity, is cast as the hero.

The means by which education improves life outcomes are varied. Certainly schooling can enhance skills that are directly used in the workplace, thereby making workers more productive. But it can also have an impact on less tangible personal attributes, and Chatterjee emphasises the qualities of integrity and assiduousness that his schooling developed in Madhav.

From George Eliot: The Mill on the Floss

"Tom," she said, timidly, when they were out of doors, "how much money did you give for your rabbits?"

"Two half-crowns and a sixpence," said Tom, promptly.

"I think I've got a great deal more than that in my steel purse upstairs. I'll ask mother to give it you."

"What for?" said Tom. "I don't want *your* money, you silly thing. I've got a great deal more money than you, because I'm a boy. I always have half-sovereigns and sovereigns for my Christmas boxes because I shall be a man, and you only have five-shilling pieces, because you're only a girl."

In this section, Maggie offers her brother, Tom, some money. But it is clear that he receives favourable treatment simply by virtue of being a boy. Discrimination of this kind often extends to the market for labour. As we have seen competition between employers should ensure that workers are paid according to how productive they are. If women and men are equally productive but the former are paid less than the latter, then this poses a puzzle—why would new employers not set themselves up that increased the pay offered to women, attracting women from the discriminating employer? Competition ought to eradicate discrimination. But social norms can be strong, and so discrimination exists in spite of this competition.

Consider the market for superstars. Top sportspeople or entertainers can earn huge salaries. Why is this? Is it fair?

Chapter 8
Externalities—Greta's Expectations

From Thomas Hardy: Jude the Obscure

On a Monday morning the chairman of the school committee called, and after attending to the business of the school drew Phillotson aside out of earshot of the children.

"You'll excuse my asking, Phillotson, since everybody is talking of it: is this true as to your domestic affairs—that your wife's going away was on no visit, but a secret elopement with a lover? If so, I condole with you."

"Don't," said Phillotson. "There was no secret about it."

"She has gone to visit friends?"

"No."

"Then what has happened?"

"She has gone away under circumstances that usually call for condolence with the husband. But I gave my consent."

The chairman looked as if he had not apprehended the remark.

"What I say is quite true," Phillotson continued testily. "She asked leave to go away with her lover, and I let her. Why shouldn't I? A woman of full age, it was a question of her own conscience—not for me. I was not her gaoler. I can't explain any further. I don't wish to be questioned."

The children observed that much seriousness marked the faces of the two men, and went home and told their parents that something new had happened about Mrs. Phillotson. Then Phillotson's little maidservant, who was a schoolgirl just out of her standards, said that Mr. Phillotson had helped in his wife's packing, had offered her what money she required, and had written a friendly letter to her young man, telling him to take care of her. The chairman of committee thought the matter over, and talked to the other managers of the school, till a request came to Phillotson to meet them privately. The meeting lasted a long time, and at the end the school-master came home, looking as usual pale and worn. Gillingham was sitting in his house awaiting him.

© The Author(s), under exclusive license to Springer Nature Switzerland AG 2023   43
G. Johnes, *Economics for Lovers of Literature*,
https://doi.org/10.1007/978-3-031-26486-3_8

"Well; it is as you said," observed Phillotson, flinging himself down wearily in a chair. "They have requested me to send in my resignation on account of my scandalous conduct in giving my tortured wife her liberty—or, as they call it, condoning her adultery. But I shan't resign!"

"I think I would."

"I won't. It is no business of theirs. It doesn't affect me in my public capacity at all. They may expel me if they like."

"If you make a fuss it will get into the papers, and you'll never get appointed to another school. You see, they have to consider what you did as done by a teacher of youth—and its effects as such upon the morals of the town; and, to ordinary opinion, your position is indefensible. You must let me say that."

To this good advice, however, Phillotson would not listen.

"I don't care," he said. "I don't go unless I am turned out. And for this reason; that by resigning I acknowledge I have acted wrongly by her; when I am more and more convinced every day that in the sight of Heaven and by all natural, straightforward humanity, I have acted rightly."

Gillingham saw that his rather headstrong friend would not be able to maintain such a position as this; but he said nothing further, and in due time—indeed, in a quarter of an hour—the formal letter of dismissal arrived.

Themes of constraints imposed by social morality and social divisions run through Hardy's Jude the Obscure. Each of the central characters, Jude and Sue, has a romantic history that is (to put it mildly) tangled. When they finally get together, it seems that they have reached the right outcome. But their union has an effect on others—and here is the link to the theme of this chapter. When people's actions have an impact on others, and they make no allowance for this in their decision-making, the decisions that they make may not be the best decisions for society as a whole. In this respect, Jude and Sue's actions are somewhat similar to those of the young lady who sat opposite me on a train as I was reading the book—when she tucked into a pack of sushi, I couldn't work out whether I was offended by the smell or jealous, but it certainly had an effect on me which she didn't take into account.

In the above extract from Jude the Obscure, schoolteacher Richard Phillotson allows his wife, Sue, to leave him for Jude Fawley. What should have been a private affair had broader consequences. In some way, this adversely affected the utility of members of the school committee—presumably, they feared that Richard's actions would have adverse implications either for the moral welfare of the pupils or the school's reputation. This is a classic spillover effect, or what economists call an 'externality'. Externalities have serious implications for the operation of a free market economic system.

Ordinarily, trade between two people (or two firms, or between a person and a firm) affects just those who are directly involved. You and I made a trade when you bought this book, and hopefully, you think it is worth the money you paid. In fact, I hope you like it so much that you can't stop talking about it. That's great. It might not be so great for the people you live with, especially if they are foolish and don't enjoy economics. But you and I didn't take them into account when you bought the book—we only considered whether there was an overlap between what you were willing to pay for the book and what I would be willing to accept. Your partner didn't come into it. You and I were made better off by the trade, but your partner may have been made worse off—so from a holistic point of view, maybe we shouldn't have traded. In the same way, Richard and Sue may not have behaved as they did had they taken the school committee's feelings on the matter into account. Had Gillingham been able to force Richard to consider the wider consequences before, rather than after, the event, who knows whether his friend would have acted as he did?

It is not difficult to think of other examples of spillover effects. The price I paid for my electric guitar did not include any allowance for the disturbance it might cause my neighbours. If I decide to take my car for a drive along a busy motorway, I may not consider the impact that my decision has on the congestion faced by other motorists. Neither might I consider the impact that my decision has on pollution. Likewise, as I pay an energy company for the heating of my house, I might not consider the wider impact of greenhouse gases. A coal-fired power station sells electricity to consumers via the grid, but may not consider the full impact of the smoke it creates.

Many of these examples have relevance for the environment. Indeed environmental problems have arisen precisely because the wider impacts of trade are not adequately considered when the trades take place. The normal rules of the market—where price is used to bring demand and supply into balance—fail to deliver an outcome that is the best for society. In this respect, spillovers are like any other type of market failure—recall that monopoly power in the market for goods and services gives a result that is less than ideal too.

The problem giving rise to spillovers is basically this: wider consequences are not considered. That is, they are not accounted for either in the demand of the buyer or the supply of the seller. One way to fix this problem is to tweak either the buyer's demand or the seller's supply by introducing a tax, payment of which encourages them to behave as if they are allowing for the wider consequences of their action. For example, introducing a congestion charge whereby drivers have to pay for access to a stretch of road would reduce demand for journeys on that road, and hence reduce the extent of congestion. Taxing fuel reduces the demand for car travel and so reduces pollution. By setting taxes of this kind at an appropriate level, governments can provide markets with a nudge so that they work better when, in the absence of government intervention, they would fail.

An alternative view is that taxes of this kind are not necessary. Let's step back from the idea that buyers and sellers fail adequately to take into account the spillover effects generated by their trade. Suppose that people who are adversely affected by these spillovers have a legal right to redress. So my neighbour could have a legal right to peace and quiet and could require me to compensate him when I play my guitar too loudly. People could have a legal right to clean air and could take polluters to court to demand compensation. If property rights were strong enough, spillovers would not be a problem. In many cases, strong property rights can therefore be a cure for market failure due to externalities. But in other cases (such as the effect that one extra car on a stretch of road has on congestion) the costs and practicalities of arranging lawsuits may mean that it makes more sense to fix the externality through the tax system.

From George Orwell—The Road to Wigan Pier

Windows which refuse to open are a peculiarity of old mining towns. Some of these towns are so undermined by ancient workings that the ground is constantly subsiding and the houses above slip sideways. In Wigan you pass whole rows of houses which have slid to startling angles, their windows being ten or twenty degrees out of the horizontal. Sometimes the front wall bellies outward till it looks as though the house were seven months gone in pregnancy. It can be refaced, but the new facing soon begins to bulge again. When a house sinks at all suddenly its windows are jammed for ever and the door has to be refitted. This excites no surprise locally.

The operations of the mining companies documented by Orwell have a profound effect on householders if subsidence damages their homes. If the householders have strong legal rights, then they could presumably claim compensation from the mining companies, if necessary through the courts. But if those legal rights are weak—if, for example, the mining companies are no longer in business—the byproduct of the companies' business decisions is an adverse impact that, in the absence of compensation from another source, seems unjust.

An extreme kind of spillover effect concerns the provision of certain services. National security is something—the clue is in the name—that can only be provided to everyone in the nation or to nobody. This applies to the armed forces and also to espionage activity, all of which protect us from foreign threats. If these services are to be provided to just one person in the country, they must be provided to all. The important characteristic of these services is that they are not privately consumed—one person enjoying these services does not mean that they are unavailable to others, but on the contrary means that they have to be consumed by others. Services of this kind tend to be provided by government, because (as a consequence of extreme market failure) it would otherwise be impossible to evaluate how much each individual in society is willing to pay. Other examples of these types of services, or 'public goods', include street lighting, maintenance of public areas.

In the last few chapters, we've examined a number of sources of market failure—monopoly power, institutions in the labour market, externalities and public goods. Market failure is not always a bad thing. Spillover effects can be positive rather than negative, especially if my neighbour likes my guitar playing. The institutions of the labour market exist largely because they are welfare-enhancing. But, whether the effects are negative or positive, any case where the forces of demand and supply does not result in an outcome that maximises surpluses is an example of the invisible hand failing properly to guide the economy. The question of how important these market failures are in practice brings to mind the question: how long is a piece of string? Whether they lead to a substantial or trivial loss of economic welfare depends in large part on people's definitions of big and small. Measuring helps, and a lot of economists' work is about putting numbers on the impact of market failures. But even when we can put a value on what we, as a society, lose due to monopoly power or union power, or negative environmental spillovers, people view that valuation from different perspectives. So people differ in their ideas about whether governments (which are themselves imperfect) should intervene and act to resolve market failures, or whether to leave well alone.

Climate change is expected to impact severely future generations. To what extent should we take those generations into account in our decision-making? What incentives can the authorities put in place for people to behave in ways that are more environmentally friendly?

Chapter 9
International Trade—Why Trade Is Good: Part 2

From George Eliot: The Mill on the Floss

If such were the views of life on which the Dodsons and Tullivers had been reared in the praiseworthy past of Pitt and high prices, you will infer from what you already know concerning the state of society in St Ogg's, that there had been no highly modifying influence to act on them in their maturer life.

Maggie Tulliver is the main protagonist in The Mill on the Floss. The book follows her life, troubled by financial concerns surrounding Dorlcote Mill, the family business, and also by her romantic liaisons—which grow increasingly complex and are ultimately resolved only... ah, but that would be a spoiler. It is an exceptionally rich book, particularly for an economist to read. The above quote is an aside, but an important one. The 'praiseworthy past' of 'high prices' refers to a debate that was virulent in British politics in the mid-1840s, around 15 years before the publication Eliot's novel. In 1846, the Corn Laws, which allowed tariffs to be levied on imported foodstuffs, were repealed. These had been introduced to finance the Napoleonic wars, and (as well as producing tax revenue for the government) had served to protect domestic producers from foreign competition. Producers in Britain could therefore compete effectively, even though their costs, and so also their prices were higher than those of foreign producers. The domestic producers of course welcomed the high prices, but there are downsides—not least, domestic consumers had to pay more. While I was reading this book, I had a local company around to give me an estimate for replacing the front and back doors of my house. They quoted over £8000 for two doors! Sure, they're bespoke, handcrafted and locally produced. Somehow, I think I'll be going for a mass-produced imported option.

Fast forward to 2016, when Donald Trump won the US presidential election with a slogan and commitment to put 'America first'. He introduced taxes (known as tariffs) on various imported goods, such as washing machines and solar panels, and also brought in tariffs aimed specifically at particular countries, notably China. These moves were opposed by some, but supported by others—notably trade unions, which perceived that the tariffs protected their members' jobs. The whole purpose of tariffs

© The Author(s), under exclusive license to Springer Nature Switzerland AG 2023
G. Johnes, *Economics for Lovers of Literature*,
https://doi.org/10.1007/978-3-031-26486-3_9

is, of course, to make imported goods more expensive so that domestically produced goods are made relatively cheaper. This gives the domestically produced goods a leg-up, hence supporting the firms that produce them and supporting also employment in those firms. As well as to fund the war effort, it was precisely to support agricultural activity that the Corn Laws were introduced. And it was to support employment in depressed areas of the US that Trump imposed his tariffs.

Making imports more expensive relative to domestically produced goods involves a deliberate distortion of market signals. Where markets work well, prices serve as a guide to the real cost (in terms of resources) of production. If one country can produce a product more cheaply than can another country, then presumably the first country has some kind of advantage in producing that product. Usually this is a question of resources. The country might be able to produce coal cheaply because it has large reserves of easily accessed coal underground. Or it might be able to produce grain cheaply because the country's geography is characterised by large flat areas that allow for easy agrarian farming. Or it might be able to produce software cheaply because it has large numbers of highly trained IT workers. Or it might be able to produce cars cheaply because it has previously invested heavily in robotics and has developed a supply chain of companies that can program, service and maintain the machines used in vehicle production.

If the second country imposes a tariff on, say, coal, its domestic coal producers (and their employees) will benefit. But the tariff protects relatively inefficient production. It will serve to raise output of coal in the more costly country and reduce the market for the output of the less costly country's coal producers. Across the piece, coal will be produced more expensively, on average, than is the case without the tariff. This means that (at the global level) more resources are needed to produce a certain amount of coal when the tariff is in place than when it is not. More people need to be employed to produce the coal. And that means that fewer people are available to be employed doing other things—where they might be more productive. Ideally, therefore, loosely speaking, the places best equipped to produce coal should produce coal, and other places should produce other things. And trade.

This seems to shock some people. People who, without a thought, buy a newspaper (rather than lurking on Twitter), or a coffee (rather than making it themselves), or a bag of flour (rather than growing the corn and milling it) find the idea of trade strange—even though they are doing it themselves all the time. In our daily lives we tend to specialise in something so that we get really good at it, sell it in return for a wage, and then use that wage to buy things that we're not so good at doing. Actually, we go a little further: if we can earn a high wage doing something, we may hire someone to do some menial tasks for us rather than doing them perfectly well ourselves. That's because we're better off concentrating on the high-wage activity. Every day, we make decisions about what to produce ourselves and what to acquire through trade on the basis of comparative advantage. The thing that people find strange is the idea that the same principle applies at the level of an entire country. But it does.

Austenasia is a micronation formed when a father and son (the Austen family) declared independence from the UK, a declaration that the UK government treated with the contempt it (probably quite rightly) thought it deserved. The Austens presumably trade with the UK, and no one would find that surprising. They need to buy their beer from somewhere. Likewise the, somewhat larger, UK trades with other countries. Famously, Twitter user @FleetwoodTerryO expressed amazement and disgust that Yorkshire tea is not, in fact, produced in Yorkshire but comes from Africa and India. Those familiar with Yorkshire—its weather conditions and the clay soil with poor drainage—will know that it is far from ideal for growing the Camellias used to make tea. Trade makes good sense. It makes sense also for things other than tea—things that could in principle be produced anywhere. Buying a car made in Korea is not an act of disloyalty or treason—it is simply a recognition that Koreans produce cars, other countries produce other stuff, and we can make an exchange that is mutually beneficial.

Putting barriers in the way of that exchange is not beneficial. Tariffs are one type of trade barrier, but there are others. Regulations, for example, health and safety regulations relating to the design of products, the quality of foodstuffs, or the qualifications of workers providing services, can often be used to restrict trade. To be sure, health and safety should be safeguarded, but the danger exists that regulations of this kind go beyond such safeguarding and are used instead to impede trade.

While, overall, trade with other countries is beneficial, and restricting trade is harmful, we should bear in mind that it does not impact everyone in the same way. The benefits of trade more than offset the costs, but at the level of the individual business or the individual worker experiences may differ. This is why the unions were supportive of Trump's tariffs—the tariffs helped those particular workers. They did not help the customers of those workers' firms, who had to pay more for their products. In an ideal world, the winners from free trade could compensate the losers with some room to spare. But it's important to recognise that arrangements are not usually made to ensure that the winners do in practice compensate the losers—and that is why some groups still advocate for trade restrictions.

The word 'trade' implies that one thing is traded for another. If one country imports something from another country, then the trade implies that something goes the other way. Generally speaking, things do. But, recognising that the world is made up of many countries, the trading relationship may not be a simple one. The UK may buy cars from Korea and not sell anything directly in return. But the UK may produce pharmaceuticals that it sells to India, and India may sell software to Korea. Clearly the important thing is that, overall, the value of imports (from all foreign countries together) should balance the value of exports (to all countries together). When that is the case, our country is 'paying its way'.

In any one year, however, it is possible that this balance is not observed. A country may sell more to other countries than it buys from them over the course of a year. Or it may buy more than it sells. This is normal—after all, the businesses that import things into this country are not in some mysterious way coordinated with the businesses that export. When a firm imports things, it uses money (not goods) to pay for them. Likewise, when a firm exports, it receives money. If you work for a firm that imports raw materials from, say, Chile, then someone in your firm will have to exchange currency for Chilean pesos, and then trade these for the raw materials. If your British firm then sells its output to a firm in China, the Chinese firm will need to convert its renminbi into pounds in order to pay you for what it is buying.

If, across all transactions made between firms and individuals in the domestic economy in a particular year, the value of imports exceeds the value of exports, then there is a transfer of financial assets out of the domestic economy. One very simple way of looking at this is to think of the money being paid to the firms from which we import as an asset. It is an IOU. It is a claim on our economy that can be put into effect at some later date. In fact, the payment does not have to be made using money (at least not in a narrow sense). Any kind of financial asset that can be thought of as an IOU can be used to bring the international books into balance. So the financial assets traded across nations could include securities such as government bonds. These will be valued by foreign individuals, businesses, and governments so long as they have confidence in the future of the domestic economy. This means that a deficit in trade of tangible goods and services can be financed by a surplus on trade in financial assets.

A deficit on trade of tangibles does, if sustained over a long period of time, have adverse consequences though. If domestic firms are demanding a lot of foreign currency in order to pay for imports, while foreign firms are not demanding much of our domestic currency because we are not exporting so much, that has implications for the price of currency. Demand for our domestic currency will be relatively weak, and so the price of that currency (as measured in terms of foreign currency) will tend to fall. If we are in the UK, this means that the value of the pound in terms of other currencies goes down. We, therefore, have to pay more pounds in order to buy a dollar, or a peso, or a renminbi. And people in other countries need to pay less of their own currency in order to buy a pound. Over time, this makes it more expensive for people in the UK to buy foreign goods and services (because we have to pay more pounds to buy a dollar's worth of goods). And it makes it cheaper for people elsewhere to buy UK-produced stuff. This means that the imbalance between imports and exports is self-correcting. For a country that has not been exporting as much as it has been importing, that self-correction can be quite painful, because it involves rising prices. But over time, this mechanism means that countries must pay their way.

At the end of Shirley, Charlotte Bronte talks of the effects of removing the blockade on trade that had been imposed during the Napoleonic Wars. The resultant boost to the economy was dramatic:

On the 18th of June 1812 the Orders in Council were repealed, and the blockaded ports thrown open. You know very well—such of you as are old enough to remember- you made Yorkshire and Lancashire shake with your shout on that occasion. The ringers cracked a bell in Briarfield belfry; it is dissonant to this day. The Association of Merchants and Manufacturers dined together at Stilbro', and one and all went home in such a plight as their wives would never wish to witness more. Liverpool started and snorted like a river-horse roused amongst his reeds by thunder. Some of the American merchants felt threatenings of apoplexy, and had themselves bled—all, like wise men, at this first moment of prosperity, prepared to rush into the bowels of speculation,

and to delve new difficulties, in whose depths they might lose themselves at some future day. Stocks which had been accumulating for years now went off in a moment, in the twinkling of an eye. Warehouses were lightened, ships were laden; work abounded, wages rose; the good time seemed come. These prospects might be delusive, but they were brilliant—to some they were even true. At that epoch, in that single month of June, many a solid fortune was realized.

The exchange rate at which one country's currency is converted to another's may, as we have seen, rise or fall with changes in economic conditions. In The Innocents Abroad, Mark Twain tells an amusing story of events that befell him in the Azores:

The Portuguese pennies, or reis (pronounced rays), are prodigious. It takes one thousand reis to make a dollar, and all financial estimates are made in reis. We did not know this until after we had found it out through Blucher. Blucher said he was so happy and so grateful to be on solid land once more that he wanted to give a feast—said he had heard it was a cheap land, and he was bound to have a grand banquet. He invited nine of us, and we ate an excellent dinner at the principal hotel. In the midst of the jollity produced by good cigars, good wine, and passable anecdotes, the landlord presented his bill. Blucher glanced at it and his countenance fell. He took another look to assure himself that his senses had not deceived him and then read the items aloud, in a faltering voice, while the roses in his cheeks turned to ashes:

"'Ten dinners, at 600 reis, 6,000 reis!' Ruin and desolation!

"'Twenty-five cigars, at 100 reis, 2,500 reis!' Oh, my sainted mother!

"'Eleven bottles of wine, at 1,200 reis, 13,200 reis!' Be with us all!

"'TOTAL, TWENTY-ONE THOUSAND SEVEN HUNDRED REIS!' The suffering Moses! There ain't money enough in the ship to pay that bill! Go—leave me to my misery, boys, I am a ruined community."

I think it was the blankest-looking party I ever saw. Nobody could say a word. It was as if every soul had been stricken dumb. Wine glasses descended slowly to the table, their contents untasted. Cigars dropped unnoticed from nerveless fingers. Each man sought his neighbor's eye, but found in it no ray of hope, no encouragement. At last the fearful silence was broken. The shadow of a desperate resolve settled upon Blucher's countenance like a cloud, and he rose up and said:

"Landlord, this is a low, mean swindle, and I'll never, never stand it. Here's a hundred and fifty dollars, Sir, and it's all you'll get—I'll swim in blood before I'll pay a cent more."

Our spirits rose and the landlord's fell—at least we thought so; he was confused, at any rate, notwithstanding he had not understood a word that had been said. He glanced from the little pile of gold pieces to Blucher several times and then went out. He must have visited an American, for when he returned, he brought back his bill translated into a language that a Christian could understand—thus:

10 dinners, 6000 reis, or	$6.00
25 cigars, 2500 reis, or	$2.50
11 bottles wine, 13,200 reis, or	$13.20
Total 21,700 reis, or	$21.70

Happiness reigned once more in Blucher's dinner party. More refreshments were ordered.

Clearing up such misunderstandings is obviously essential for trade and for happiness.

Consider how the benefits of international trade have led to the development of agreements between countries such as the European Union, the African Continental Free Trade Area, and the Association of South-East Asian Nations.

Chapter 10
Information Economics—Well, What Do You Know?

From Charles Dickens: Nicholas Nickleby

'I have ventured to call, ma'am,' said Kate, after a few seconds of awkward silence, 'from having seen your advertisement.'

'Yes,' replied Mrs. Wititterly, 'one of my people put it in the paper—Yes.'

'I thought, perhaps,' said Kate, modestly, 'that if you had not already made a final choice, you would forgive my troubling you with an application.'

'Yes,' drawled Mrs. Wititterly again.

'If you have already made a selection—'

'Oh dear no,' interrupted the lady, 'I am not so easily suited. I really don't know what to say. You have never been a companion before, have you?'

Mrs. Nickleby, who had been eagerly watching her opportunity, came dexterously in, before Kate could reply. 'Not to any stranger, ma'am,' said the good lady; 'but she has been a companion to me for some years. I am her mother, ma'am.'

'Oh!' said Mrs. Wititterly, 'I apprehend you.'

'I assure you, ma'am,' said Mrs. Nickleby, 'that I very little thought, at one time, that it would be necessary for my daughter to go out into the world at all, for her poor dear papa was an independent gentleman, and would have been at this moment if he had but listened in time to my constant entreaties and—'

'Dear mama,' said Kate, in a low voice.

'My dear Kate, if you will allow me to speak,' said Mrs. Nickleby, 'I shall take the liberty of explaining to this lady—'

'I think it is almost unnecessary, mama.'

And notwithstanding all the frowns and winks with which Mrs. Nickleby intimated that she was going to say something which would clench the business at once, Kate maintained her point by an expressive look, and for once Mrs. Nickleby was stopped upon the very brink of an oration.

'What are your accomplishments?' asked Mrs. Wititterly, with her eyes shut.

G. Johnes, *Economics for Lovers of Literature*,
https://doi.org/10.1007/978-3-031-26486-3_10

Kate blushed as she mentioned her principal acquirements, and Mrs. Nickleby checked them all off, one by one, on her fingers; having calculated the number before she came out. Luckily the two calculations agreed, so Mrs. Nickleby had no excuse for talking.

'You are a good temper?' asked Mrs. Wititterly, opening her eyes for an instant, and shutting them again.

'I hope so,' rejoined Kate.

'And have a highly respectable reference for everything, have you?'

Kate replied that she had, and laid her uncle's card upon the table.

'Have the goodness to draw your chair a little nearer, and let me look at you,' said Mrs. Wititterly; 'I am so very nearsighted that I can't quite discern your features.'

Kate complied, though not without some embarrassment, with this request, and Mrs. Wititterly took a languid survey of her countenance, which lasted some two or three minutes.

'I like your appearance,' said that lady, ringing a little bell. 'Alphonse, request your master to come here.'

The page disappeared on this errand, and after a short interval, during which not a word was spoken on either side, opened the door for an important gentleman of about eight-and-thirty, of rather plebeian countenance, and with a very light head of hair, who leant over Mrs. Wititterly for a little time, and conversed with her in whispers.

'Oh!' he said, turning round, 'yes. This is a most important matter. Mrs Wititterly is of a very excitable nature; very delicate, very fragile; a hothouse plant, an exotic.'

'Oh! Henry, my dear,' interposed Mrs. Wititterly.

'You are, my love, you know you are; one breath—' said Mr. W., blowing an imaginary feather away. 'Pho! you're gone!'

The lady sighed.

Nicholas Nickleby is one of the greatest of Charles Dickens's novels. There are in fact two Nicholas Nicklebys—father and son. The father was one of two brothers—the other being Ralph. When Nicholas senior died, Nicholas junior (and his sister and mother) fell into Ralph's care. But Ralph was not very caring. The story focuses on how life evolves for young Nicholas—alongside Kate (his sister), Smike (his lackey/ friend/mystery), and other characters—and on how Ralph gets his comeuppance. It is a story that is full of unknowns. If characters had full information, things would not pan out as they did. But of course, we don't always have full information. Indeed, had I known everything about some of the books quoted in this volume before reading them, I probably wouldn't have read them! Nicholas Nickleby, I should add, is definitely one to read.

Competition between providers of goods and services is a powerful means of ensuring that society's goals are met. If buyers know where they can obtain things at the cheapest price, they will flock to those providers offering the best deals. But if they don't have this information, their welfare can be compromised. So information is critical to the smooth operation of an economy. But very often the reality is that not everyone has access to full information. Where they don't, information becomes highly valuable.

There are several ways in which deficient information can frustrate the smooth operation of the economy. This episode from Nicholas Nickleby describes a fairly standard job interview—one where inevitably the interviewee, Kate, knows more about herself than does the interviewer, Mrs. Wititterly. The interview itself is a process in which Mrs. Wititterly tries to gather information. Moreover, in seeking a reference from Kate's uncle, Mrs. Wititterly hopes to confirm that Kate does indeed have the attributes that she deems necessary for the job. The situation, then, is one where the seller, Kate, has information about the quality of what she is selling—her own labour—that the buyer does not have.[1]

A similar scenario presents itself when second-hand goods, such as used cars, are being sold. Someone selling a car knows well the shortcomings of the vehicle, but prospective purchasers do not have this information. In some situations, this can lead to an unravelling of the whole market. Since buyers don't have full information, they must proceed on an assumption about the quality of the car—they might, for example, suppose that, beyond the quality of the bodywork and other things that they can easily check, the car is of average quality. For sellers of particularly good quality vehicles, the price that buyers offer might not be high enough to compensate them for losing such a good car. So the cars that are put on the market are likely to be at the lower end of the quality range—'bangers' or 'lemons'. Buyers might then take this into account, and be reluctant to buy. In extreme cases, the whole market for used products collapses. There are, of course, solutions to this problem, and this is why it is common for used cars to be sold with a warranty.

Another character in Nicholas Nickleby is Alfred Muntle (also known as Mr. Mantalini). A reckless spendthrift, he unsurprisingly fails to recognise a 'lemon' when considering the purchase of a horse.

'You can't want any more just now,' said Madame coaxingly.

'My life and soul,' returned her husband, 'there is a horse for sale at Scrubbs's, which it would be a sin and a crime to lose—going, my senses' joy, for nothing.'

'For nothing,' cried Madame, 'I am glad of that.'

'For actually nothing,' replied Mantalini. 'A hundred guineas down will buy him; mane, and crest, and legs, and tail, all of the demdest beauty. I will ride him in the park before the very chariots of the rejected countesses. The demd old dowager will faint with grief and rage; the other two will say "He is married, he has made away with himself, it is a demd thing, it is all up!" They will hate each other demnebly, and wish you dead and buried. Ha! ha! Demmit.'

Madame Mantalini's prudence, if she had any, was not proof against these triumphal pictures.

Returning to Mrs. Wititterly, her search for a paid companion is, like many examples where employers are looking for new hires and workers are looking for new

---

[1] This situation, where the lack of information on one side of a market biases the quality of the offering that is made to the market, is sometimes referred to as 'adverse selection'.

employment, a task that is undertaken sequentially—that is, she samples one prospective employee after another. This type of search, which necessarily involves imperfect information, is typical of many contexts, and is well understood by Violet Effingham—a character in Trollope's book Phineas Finn—who discusses the search for a husband with her friend Lady Laura Standish.

Laura got up and came to the sofa, and sat close to her friend. Violet, though she somewhat moved one foot, so as to seem to make room for the other, still went on with her play.

"If you do marry, Violet, you must choose some one man out of the lot."

"That's quite true, my dear, I certainly can't marry them all."

"And how do you mean to make the choice?"

"I don't know. I suppose I shall toss up."

"I wish you would be in earnest with me."

"Well;—I will be in earnest. I shall take the first that comes after I have quite made up my mind. You'll think it very horrible, but that is really what I shall do. After all, a husband is very much like a house or a horse. You don't take your house because it's the best house in the world, but because just then you want a house. You go and see a house, and if it's very nasty you don't take it. But if you think it will suit pretty well, and if you are tired of looking about for houses, you do take it. That's the way one buys one's horses,—and one's husbands."

No doubt, Mrs. Wititterly was unlikely to employ the first applicant that she interviewed for the post of paid companion. But neither was she likely to continue the search indefinitely. At some point, she would balance the costs and benefits of prolonging the search and would decide that the most recent interviewee would do.

In the same way, Kate Nickleby is unlikely to have lacked other job opportunities, and she would make a decision about accepting or rejecting Mrs. Wititterly's offer on the basis of balancing the benefits of taking the job—whatever wage is offered—against those of prolonging her search—the possibility (and, given limited information, it is only a possibility) of securing a higher wage elsewhere, taking into account also the costs of staying out of work a bit longer. This means that, in a world of imperfect information, unemployment can be a good thing; staying unemployed and searching for a better-paying job is, in effect, an investment in one's own future. Unemployment is not *necessarily* a bad thing—though prolonged unemployment and high levels of overall joblessness are of course likely to be bad.

Elsewhere in Nicholas Nickleby, there are examples of different types of issues that can arise from imperfect information. At the very start of the book, Godfrey Nickleby (father of Nicholas senior) considers a rather drastic solution to his family's poverty.

At length, after five years, when Mrs. Nickleby had presented her husband with a couple of sons, and that embarrassed gentleman, impressed with the necessity of making some provision for his family, was seriously revolving in his mind a little commercial speculation of insuring his life next quarter-day,

and then falling from the top of the Monument by accident, there came, one morning, by the general post, a black-bordered letter to inform him how his uncle, Mr. Ralph Nickleby, was dead, and had left him the bulk of his little property, amounting in all to five thousand pounds sterling.

Godfrey would have information that his insurers would not—namely that he intended to behave in such a way that precipitated a payout. Insurance exists as a means of protecting people from losses that are due to unforeseen events. So it's possible to insure against illness, or accident, or against being the victim of crime, or—as in Godfrey's case—against one's own death. In effect, insurance is a bet—by buying insurance, one is betting that something bad will happen and necessitate a payout that offsets the cost of the premiums paid to the insurer. By selling insurance, the insurer bets that this will not happen. The problem arises when someone who has bought insurance can affect the outcome. If the buyer does this, he or she has information that the insurer does not have, and that can be a problem. In Godfrey's case, he intended to end his life deliberately and trigger a pay out for his family. Clearly, if the insurer knew that this was in Godfrey's mind, it would not engage in the bet. For precisely this reason, life insurance is typically voided in cases of suicide.

Less extreme examples are relevant too. By buying insurance, people may take less care. They may be less likely to check that they have locked all doors and windows, or switched off the oven or fire, before leaving their home. Insurance companies need to bear this in mind when they provide their services, and put conditions in place to ensure that their customers behave responsibly. Nevertheless, the absence of full information leaves scope for the market to fail. In extreme cases, this might lead to a market for insurance failing altogether. During the COVID-19 pandemic, it was impossible to buy insurance for travel that was disrupted by the need for people to self-isolate, simply because it was impossible for insurance companies to verify the requirement for self-isolation.

Imperfect competition compromises the effectiveness of the free market in securing the best possible outcomes because sellers face incentives not to cut price to sell to some prospective buyers who are willing to pay more than the costs of production. The interdependence of people likewise compromises the free market because the actions of one person can sometimes adversely affect other people without any compensation. Imperfect information adds to the catalogue of things that can lead to a free market producing less than perfect outcomes. If a used car market cannot exist because people fear buying 'lemons', or if an insurance market cannot exist because insurance companies fear being cheated, then the market is clearly failing. Of course, it is possible for mitigations to be put in place, but these are themselves imperfect. The idea of a world that can operate perfectly when left to its own devices is just that—an idea, or, rather, an ideal. The real world is dirtier than that. Interfering with the dirty real world might improve things—but it might not. Rather than reasoning in the abstract, understanding the economy requires us to look at the data and examine what really goes on in the world.

Since poor information can lead to poor decisions, consider how flows of information could be improved in markets with which you are familiar. What would be the benefits?

Chapter 11
Behavioural Economics—Don't Behave Like That

From Oscar Wilde—The Picture of Dorian Gray

There are moments, psychologists tell us, when the passion for sin, or for what the world calls sin, so dominates a nature that every fibre of the body, as every cell of the brain, seems to be instinct with fearful impulses. Men and women at such moments lose the freedom of their will. They move to their terrible end as automatons move. Choice is taken from them, and conscience is either killed, or, if it lives at all, lives but to give rebellion its fascination and disobedience its charm. For all sins, as theologians weary not of reminding us, are sins of disobedience.

The Picture of Dorian Gray is a remarkable book, and Wilde's only novel. It is based on a surreal deal struck by the main protagonist that allows him not to age. The above quotation refers to a vicious physical attack by James Vane on Dorian Gray—an attack that would not have taken place if Vane had made full use of the information available to him (though it might have had he known that Gray could not age). It brings to mind the plethora of economic decisions that we make without taking on board all the information that we have. As the psychologists mentioned by Wilde suggest, our behaviour is not always rational—and that is a challenge to a lot of conventional economic theory, since that fundamentally assumes that people behave rationally. Maybe irrationality explains my choice of which football team to support. Elsewhere in Wilde's novel, Lord Henry observes:

What absurd fellows you are, both of you! I wonder who it was defined man as a rational animal. It was the most premature definition ever given. Man is many things, but he is not rational. I am glad he is not, after all—though I wish you chaps would not squabble over the picture. You had much better let me have it, Basil. This silly boy doesn't really want it, and I really do.

The idea of rationality has been fundamental to everything discussed in this book so far. Individuals are assumed to pursue their own objectives, and businesses are assumed to pursue their own profits—and the choices that they make are supposed to be the ones that best serve their pursuits. But if, as Lord Henry postulates, people are

© The Author(s), under exclusive license to Springer Nature Switzerland AG 2023

G. Johnes, *Economics for Lovers of Literature*,
https://doi.org/10.1007/978-3-031-26486-3_11

not rational, then inferring their behaviour from their objectives becomes hazardous. Nevertheless, the ways in which people are irrational might be predictable, and a lot of recent work in economics draws on insights from psychology to focus on these behavioural issues.

For sure, decisions can be difficult. Making the best decision may require information that is not easy to obtain. In particular, some of the factors that might influence our decisions might depend on what other people might choose to do in the future. While—as in the case of an industry comprised of a few firms—it might be possible to second-guess, this is not always so. So full information is not available. Indeed if full information ever were available, a decision-maker might feel unable to process it all. Often, either because of a lack of data or because there is too much of it, making decisions is about applying rules of thumb. Some of these rules of thumb, or heuristics, may be simpler than others, but whenever a decision-maker uses them, he or she is rational only in a bounded sense—the decision-maker is balancing the costs of using all the information against the benefits, coming to a decision that may not actually be the best were all information free to use.

A little introspection reveals that we use these rules of thumb all the time. In crossing a road, we do not explicitly estimate the speed of approaching cars and do the necessary calculus to see if we can cross safely. We approximate and make the judgement intuitively. In choosing to buy a bag of salt in the supermarket, we do not usually compare reviews of all brands and weigh up the reviews against any price differences—salt is a cheap product and we just pick up a bag without worrying about the difference a few pennies might make. If we were buying an expensive item such as a car, we would likely be much more considered in our approach.

People tend to regret losses more than they appreciate gains. If someone wins a bet, they feel good. They are better off than they were before. But if they lose, they feel worse off—partly because they have lost out financially, but maybe also because they feel disappointed in having made a bad bet so that their judgement is challenged. Psychologists have refined this idea, and have found a lot of evidence to suggest that the reference point is important—if people gain relative to some reference point, they feel good, but if they lose relative to that same reference point they feel bad… and they feel the loss more acutely than they enjoy the gain.

This means that the reference point—how the opportunity to make a decision is framed—is crucial. Another context in which this has been studied involves studying bets that people might or might not be willing to make. It turns out that people make the most peculiar decisions.[1]

Imagine that someone comes up to you and gives you the chance to play a game. You must choose between one of two options. Option A gives you £1,000,000 with certainty. Option B gives you £1,000,000 with a probability of 89%, £5,000,000 with a probability of 10% and zero with a probability of 1%. Faced with these options,

---

[1] The example that follows was first studied by Maurice Allais (1953) Le comportement de l'homme rationnel devant le risque: critique des postulats et axiomes de l'école Américaine, Econometrica, 21, 503–546. It has subsequently come to be known as the Allais paradox.

experimental evidence suggests that most people go for option A. The risk, however small, of ending up with nothing puts them off option B.

Now consider another game. Again you have to choose between two options. Option A gives you an 11% chance of receiving £1,000,000, but if you don't win this you get nothing. Option B gives you a 10% chance of receiving £5,000,000, but if you don't win this you get nothing. In this case, most people go for option B. Of course, framed in this way, the game leaves you with a chance of getting nothing whichever option you choose.

The weird thing is this: even though people typically opt for A in the first game and B in the second game, the fact is that we should expect a rational person to go for the same option in the second game as they do in the first game. To see this, note that option A in the first game can be represented as an 89% chance of winning £1,000,000 and an 11% chance of winning £1,000,000; note also that option B in the second game can be represented as an 89% chance of winning nothing, a 1% chance of winning nothing, and a 10% chance of winning £5,000,000. When presented in this way, it becomes clear that, in the first game, both options offer an 89% chance of winning £1,000,000, so this part of the comparison across the two options can be ignored. Likewise, in the second game, both options offer an 89% chance of winning nothing, and so this part of the comparison across these two options can be ignored. Consequently, the two games are in fact identical to each other—both of them simply involve comparing an 11% chance of winning £1,000,000 with a 1% chance of winning nothing and a 10% chance of winning £5,000,000. So it is incongruous to find that the option that people usually choose differs across these two identical games.

This lends further support to the idea that it matters how choices are presented to people—their choice will often depend critically on how the problem is framed. If it were possible to frame decisions by adjusting people's reference points, it would become possible also to have an effect on their behaviour. This observation has led many observers to investigate how behaviour can be nudged in particular directions by changing the framing. This is the psychology that lies at the heart of attempts (by businesses, or governments—or even of parents when talking to their kids) to manage expectations.

At a fairly trivial level, a picture of a fly in a urinal can be used to improve men's aim. Hitting the fly feels good and missing by such a long way that you miss the urinal feels really bad. So a simple picture can be used to reduce cleaning costs in public toilets. Another example of a nudge involves hospitals sending text reminders to patients shortly before their appointments—where these reminders include a subtle reference to the cost to the health service of an appointment, recipients are less likely to be absent.

The prospect of being able to steer the actions of whole populations through providing nudges, which are often cheap to implement, has led to many governments setting up research units that can develop new ways of influencing behaviour. Where the objective is good, that is of course laudable. We should be vigilant, however, because there is potential for nudging to have a sinister side to it. After all, abandoning rationality comes, potentially at least, at a cost. Most obviously, suppose you wish to bet on the outcome of some uncertain enterprise (a business opportunity, say); suppose further that you make the bet on instinct, while the person you bet with uses all available information. Typically (albeit not always) the other person will win the bet. By abandoning rationality, you have made yourself worse off. Silly you. But that is what we do.

Think of a time you made a decision without explicitly weighing up the economic advantages and disadvantages. What nudges might have changed your decision?

Chapter 12
Business Cycles—The Swings and Roundabouts of Outrageous Fortune

From Jane Austen: Persuasion

But now, another occupation and solicitude of mind was beginning to be added to these. Her father was growing distressed for money. She knew, that when he now took up the Baronetage, it was to drive the heavy bills of his tradespeople, and the unwelcome hints of Mr. Shepherd, his agent, from his thoughts. The Kellynch property was good, but not equal to Sir Walter's apprehension of the state required in its possessor. While Lady Elliot lived, there had been method, moderation, and economy, which had just kept him within his income; but with her had died all such right-mindedness, and from that period he had been constantly exceeding it. It had not been possible for him to spend less; he had done nothing but what Sir Walter Elliot was imperiously called on to do; but blameless as he was, he was not only growing dreadfully in debt, but was hearing of it so often, that it became vain to attempt concealing it longer, even partially, from his daughter. He had given her some hints of it the last spring in town; he had gone so far even as to say, "Can we retrench? Does it occur to you that there is any one article in which we can retrench?" and Elizabeth, to do her justice, had, in the first ardour of female alarm, set seriously to think what could be done, and had finally proposed these two branches of economy, to cut off some unnecessary charities, and to refrain from new furnishing the drawing-room; to which expedients she afterwards added the happy thought of their taking no present down to Anne, as had been the usual yearly custom. But these measures, however good in themselves, were insufficient for the real extent of the evil, the whole of which Sir Walter found himself obliged to confess to her soon afterwards. Elizabeth had nothing to propose of deeper efficacy. She felt herself ill-used and unfortunate, as did her father; and they were neither of them able to devise any means of lessening their expenses without compromising their dignity, or relinquishing their comforts in a way not to be borne.

There was only a small part of his estate that Sir Walter could dispose of; but had every acre been alienable, it would have made no difference. He had

© The Author(s), under exclusive license to Springer Nature Switzerland AG 2023
G. Johnes, *Economics for Lovers of Literature*,
https://doi.org/10.1007/978-3-031-26486-3_12

condescended to mortgage as far as he had the power, but he would never condescend to sell. No; he would never disgrace his name so far. The Kellynch estate should be transmitted whole and entire, as he had received it.

Jane Austen is the marmite of English literature. The first novel of hers that I read was the gothic parody, Northanger Abbey, and I missed the parody. (It's subtle, and I'm still far from convinced that it's actually there.) It's a book in which nothing happens, but that's the point (or at least that's what Austen fans tell me). I have never really recovered from that disappointment—not to mention the disappointment of finding that (despite a reference on the first page) the whole book isn't about playing baseball. The society she describes in her other novels seems twee and sanitised— and if I wanted to read about that, I would prefer the works of other authors such as Fanny Burney. But over time I have come to appreciate that, viewed through certain lenses, Austen's works must have been quite challenging for the time in which they were written. In particular, a feminist perspective emerges where her heroines seek to break with convention and to define their own paths through life. Austen's final novel, Persuasion, is interesting for economists not least because the story begins with an attempt by the Elliot family to reduce their outgoings by moving house. Following the Napoleonic wars the economy entered recession, and when Persuasion was published national income was some 6% lower than it had been a decade before. The loss of income meant that many families—such as the Elliots—had to reduce their outgoings, and this inevitably meant that the income of those businesses they had previously patronised was squeezed too.

From Charlotte Bronte: The Professor

I was at X—— yesterday! your brother Ned is getting richer than Croesus by railway speculations; they call him in the Piece Hall a stag of ten; and I have heard from Brown, M. and Madame Vandenhuten and Jean Baptiste talk of coming to see you next month.

The Professor was Charlotte Bronte's first novel, but was not published until after her death. While a good read, it shows some evidence of incompleteness, particularly in the rushed ending. The protagonist, William Crimsworth, is not a professor at all, but a teacher living in Belgium—hence a professeur. Interestingly, the immediate predecessor of Bronte's father as the incumbent at Haworth church was called William Grimshaw; while he did not spend time abroad (in a literal sense), his theological thinking brought him close to nonconformism, and he became a close associate of the Wesley brothers who founded Methodism. I wonder to what extent Grimshaw served as a model for Crimsworth. The reference to 'railway speculations' is particularly germane to our consideration of business cycles. During the mid-1840s many investors speculated on the stock of railway companies. This led to a boom and bust bubble, with stock prices collapsing, leaving many speculators—including the Bronte family—out of pocket.

Many of the books that gave inspiration to earlier chapters—A Tale of Two Cities, The Mill on the Floss, Shirley, Persuasion—draw heavily on the fact that there are good times and there are bad times. This is certainly true for individuals, but in these books, the individuals concerned are hit hard by adverse conditions in the broader economic environment. There are good times, when the economy as a whole is in a recovery (or boom) period, and there are bad times, with the economy falling into recession (or slump, or bust). At various times, politicians have claimed to have tamed these vicissitudes and that they have achieved an 'end to boom and bust'—but their confident proclamations have usually been followed pretty quickly by a new period of crisis. Pride comes before a fall.

To be more specific about what we mean by the terms 'recovery' and 'recession', we first need to establish a way of thinking about the economy as a whole. An obvious starting point is to measure how much income is being generated in the economy. If the total amount of income in an economy is rising, then presumably people are becoming better off. The average person has more income, so he or she can afford to buy more things that make them feel better off than they were before. (Of course, not everybody is average, and some people may be worse off while others are better off—but that's a wrinkle we'll ignore for now. Also, prices may be rising as well as incomes, and people may only feel better off if these price increases don't offset the income gains—again, we'll ignore that for now.) Adding together everybody's income needs to be done carefully. For most people, their income comes from the wages they earn by supplying their labour. But some people receive income for supplying other factors of production. For example, they may own land that they rent out. Landlords renting out apartments are an obvious example, but some rent out storage space (a garage, perhaps) or other lands (such as a field rented out to a farmer). Other income comes from the ownership of capital. Entrepreneurs may own outright the machinery that their business uses, and so they receive a payment to reward them for their investment in this equipment. Many other people own shares in companies and receive a dividend each year. If a company is profitable, it divides some of its profits amongst its shareholders as a reward for their investment in the firm and as an inducement for them to maintain their support. Many more people have savings in a bank and are paid interest on these savings. That interest comes from investments that the bank makes (including investments in businesses) and so this too represents a form of income. Adding together incomes from all sources—labour, land, capital—gives us an idea of the aggregate level of activity in an economy. It puts a value on all the work that is being done by all of the factors of production together.

But adding together all the income in an economy is only one way of calculating the national income. Another way is to add together all of the expenditure in the economy. After all, one person's expenditure is another person's income. If you buy a kebab from a street stall, your expenditure becomes income for the vendor. A third way of calculating national income is to add up the value of everything that is produced in the economy over a certain period. It is because we produce things that we can sell them and so earn an income. So national income provides us with a measure of the affluence of society, but it also measures the value of what is being produced—that is, the extent of economic activity.

Most of the time, the overall level of production (and so also of national income) grows from one year to the next. This is because we find ways of getting better at doing what we do. In particular, new ways of using technology to do work that was previously done by humans allow more to be produced with less effort. So national income tends to rise, in developed countries, by about 2% every year, simply because that is the approximate rate of technological advancement.

There is a lot of variation around this, though. During periods of recovery, national income might grow by as much as 4 or 5% over the course of a year. During a recession, it might fall by around 5% before it starts to recover again. In 2020, the national income of the UK, hit severely by the COVID-19 pandemic, fell by almost 10% before recovering sharply in 2021 after the introduction of vaccines.

The pattern of economic activity whereby national income swings between periods of recovery and of recession is known as the business cycle. In one respect, it is not at all odd that such a cycle should exist. It would be far more peculiar if national income were to grow at an absolutely steady rate with no fluctuations at all. But the long swing of the business cycle, with ups and downs happening periodically every 7–10 years or so has nevertheless attracted a lot of attention. The challenge is to explain why random fortunes and misfortunes that affect every business from time to time should have an element of synchronicity, and why the variation should be over a period of several years (rather than a few weeks or a few centuries).

There are two obvious reasons why the ups and downs should be synchronous across firms. First, they might arise from a common external shock. When, for example, a pandemic hits, it hits all firms. Secondly, firms are interconnected. This means that a drop in demand for one firm's product has knock-on effects. Firms in that company's supply chain are adversely affected. Workers may be laid off and, given their loss of earnings, will be able to spend less income on buying all sorts of other items. So the adverse blip is transmitted across the economy.

How the various random blips that affect individual businesses convert into business cycles that last several years is somewhat less clear. A moving average of a random series of numbers tends to generate long cycles. But other more fundamental economic forces might be at work. A sudden positive blip in economic activity might encourage many people to work hard in order to make hay while the sun shines, and that in itself might be sufficient to prolong the upswing. The same people might choose to exert less effort when times are not so good, and that might serve to lengthen a recession.

In Jane Austen's book, Sir Walter Elliot suffered hardship largely as a result of his own financial indiscipline following his wife's death. But the recession that followed the Napoleonic wars doubtless exacerbated his situation, forcing on his family the move out of London to Bath. In Charlotte Bronte's novel, Edward ('Ned') Crimsworth profited greatly from an upswing, specifically in the price of shares in railway companies—though as we have seen this particular boom was quickly followed by a bust.

Earlier in this chapter, we saw that the sum of all incomes should equal the sum of all expenditures in an economy; this is because, when one person spends a sum of money, someone else receives it. This simple observation has an important implication for the way in which we can picture an economy—namely, as a flow of income between different entities. Households receive income from firms to whom they supply their labour. Firms receive the expenditures of households that are buying goods and services. Income thus flows between firms and households (in the form of wages) and between households and firms (in the form of expenditures on goods and services). Firms can afford to pay as income only inasmuch as they receive expenditure on what they produce. And households can afford to spend only inasmuch as they earn an income. The total amount of income in the economy, per period of time (say, per year), is thus measured by this flow.

Once we appreciate that business cycles exist, it's appropriate to consider whether that is a good thing or a bad thing. Some degree of fluctuation is inevitable, but excessive volatility carries substantial costs. Unemployment that arises from recession brings considerable misery to the families directly affected. Meanwhile high rates of price inflation. that can result from an unchecked boom, imposes a burden on the whole population. The question arises: how can these extreme outcomes be avoided or at least moderated? What is the role of government in doing so? Answering these questions will be the focus of the next few chapters.

How can you as an individual prepare yourself for the adverse effects of a recession? How can businesses do so?

Chapter 13
Fiscal Policy—If It Moves, Tax It

From William Shakespeare: Henry VIII

> QUEEN KATHARINE. I am solicited, not by a few,
> And those of true condition, that your subjects
> Are in great grievance: there have been commissions
> Sent down among 'em which hath flaw'd the heart
> Of all their loyalties; wherein, although,
> My good Lord Cardinal, they vent reproaches
> Most bitterly on you as putter-on
> Of these exactions, yet the King our master—
> Whose honour Heaven shield from soil!—even he escapes not
> Language unmannerly; yea, such which breaks
> The sides of loyalty, and almost appears
> In loud rebellion.
> NORFOLK. Not almost appears—
> It doth appear; for, upon these taxations,
> The clothiers all, not able to maintain
> The many to them 'longing, have put off
> The spinsters, carders, fullers, weavers, who
> Unfit for other life, compell'd by hunger
> And lack of other means, in desperate manner
> Daring th' event to th' teeth, are all in uproar,
> And danger serves among them.
> KING. Taxation!
> Wherein? and what taxation? My Lord Cardinal,
> You that are blam'd for it alike with us,
> Know you of this taxation?
> WOLSEY. Please you, sir,
> I know but of a single part in aught
> Pertains to th' state, and front but in that file

G. Johnes, *Economics for Lovers of Literature*,
https://doi.org/10.1007/978-3-031-26486-3_13

Where others tell steps with me.
QUEEN KATHARINE. No, my lord!
You know no more than others! But you frame
Things that are known alike, which are not wholesome
To those which would not know them, and yet must
Perforce be their acquaintance. These exactions,
Whereof my sovereign would have note, they are
Most pestilent to th' hearing; and to bear 'em
The back is sacrifice to th' load. They say
They are devis'd by you, or else you suffer
Too hard an exclamation.
KING. Still exaction!
The nature of it? In what kind, let's know,
Is this exaction?
QUEEN KATHARINE. I am much too venturous
In tempting of your patience, but am bold'ned
Under your promis'd pardon. The subjects' grief
Comes through commissions, which compels from each
The sixth part of his substance, to be levied
Without delay; and the pretence for this
Is nam'd your wars in France. This makes bold mouths;
Tongues spit their duties out, and cold hearts freeze
Allegiance in them; their curses now
Live where their prayers did; and it's come to pass
This tractable obedience is a slave
To each incensed will. I would your Highness
Would give it quick consideration, for
There is no primer business.
KING. By my life,
This is against our pleasure.
WOLSEY. And for me,
I have no further gone in this than by
A single voice; and that not pass'd me but
By learned approbation of the judges. If I am
Traduc'd by ignorant tongues, which neither know
My faculties nor person, yet will be
The chronicles of my doing, let me say
'Tis but the fate of place, and the rough brake
That virtue must go through. We must not stint
Our necessary actions in the fear
To cope malicious censurers, which ever
As rav'nous fishes do a vessel follow
That is new-trimm'd, but benefit no further
Than vainly longing. What we oft do best,
By sick interpreters, once weak ones, is

Not ours, or not allow'd; what worst, as oft
Hitting a grosser quality, is cried up
For our best act. If we shall stand still,
In fear our motion will be mock'd or carp'd at,
We should take root here where we sit, or sit
State-statues only.
KING. Things done well
And with a care exempt themselves from fear:
Things done without example, in their issue
Are to be fear'd. Have you a precedent
Of this commission? I believe, not any.
We must not rend our subjects from our laws,
And stick them in our will. Sixth part of each?
A trembling contribution! Why, we take
From every tree lop, bark, and part o' th' timber;
And though we leave it with a root, thus hack'd,
The air will drink the sap. To every county
Where this is question'd send our letters with
Free pardon to each man that has denied
The force of this commission. Pray, look to't;
I put it to your care.
WOLSEY. [Aside to the SECRETARY] A word with you.
Let there be letters writ to every shire
Of the King's grace and pardon. The grieved commons
Hardly conceive of me—let it be nois'd
That through our intercession this revokement
And pardon comes. I shall anon advise you
Further in the proceeding.

Henry VIII was a profligate king, his military expenditure in particular putting strains on his budget that were relieved only by the imposition of taxes and a debasing of the currency that led to rampant inflation. While Shakespeare's play was written several decades after Henry's death, its first performance came within a decade of the death of his daughter (and eventual successor), Elizabeth I. At this time, taxes were required to finance the monarchy and its military endeavours. The latter may be regarded as a public good inasmuch as it provides security. As economies have developed, the range of goods the provision of which requires government support has expanded greatly, to include public health, an educated populace, and many aspects of infrastructure. Taxes have also come to be seen as one tool with which government can moderate the overall level of economic activity. Attending a performance of Henry VIII at that sad time of year when I had to fill out my tax form certainly led to a train of thought that took me well away from the play and onto less pleasurable terrain.

To depict the economy as a circular flow of income and expenditure between households and firms is, of course, a simplification. Households do not spend all of their income. They save some, and some of their income is taxed. The revenue from taxes may be used—as in Shakespeare's day—to finance military adventures, but it may also be used to provide funds for health, education, security services such as policing, commonly used services such as road construction, and a whole host of other social services. But whatever taxes are used for, they have to be paid, and that means that households' expenditure must typically be less than their income. (There are exceptions to the general rule—for instance one might take out a loan to buy a car, but one would expect later to repay that loan so that, over time, expenditure remains constrained by income.) If household expenditure is thus lower than income, firms must be receiving less as expenditure than they are paying out in income. This is obviously unsustainable unless the expenditure is supplemented by something. There are two obvious places these supplements can come from—and they mirror the destinations of household income.

Households may save by building up assets that they hold in the banking system. The banks are rewarded for their activity because they use these assets to make loans to other households and to businesses. The banks charge interest on these loans (and they may offer a somewhat lower rate of interest to people who save with the banks). By using the money that you and I have deposited at the bank in order to make loans, the bank is taking a risk. It is using its experience to make a judgement call, namely that you and I will not want to withdraw all our money from the bank at once. If we did want to do that, the bank could not repay us, because it will have loaned our money out. Normally, banks are very successful at managing this risk well.

One type of loan that banks make is a business loan. A company may wish to build a new factory or office, or buy some new machinery, and it may need a loan in order to be able to afford to do so. If one company buys a machine, another must be producing and selling it. So a loan from the banking system provides an additional source of expenditure that goes into the business sector. Firms do not only benefit from household expenditure; they benefit from expenditure of other businesses too, and that may be financed by loans. So some of what leaves households in the form of savings may get recycled by the banking sector and may return to the flow of income as a result of loans made to businesses.

The second additional source of income for firms is the government sector. Government receives income in the form of tax receipts, many of which are based on the incomes of households. It can then use this income, along with anything that it borrows, to finance its expenditure. Government expenditure includes the provision of many goods and services such as roads, emergency services, public health, and education, and also includes support provided to individuals through the welfare system. We saw earlier that we cannot necessarily rely on the free market to provide some things, particularly where spillovers are prevalent; so the provision of emergency services (where protecting one person from a riot inevitably means protecting other people too) is usually regarded as a public good, appropriately provided by government.

But the fact that the government identifies the need for a service and provides the funding for it does not imply that it is also the government that should actually provide it. It is very often the case that government funding is used to pay for activity undertaken by private sector firms. Roads are usually paid for by the government, but are built by private firms. A procurement process allows these firms to enter contracts that ensure that government spending will pay for the services that the firms provide. So government spending is another source of expenditure that businesses can access.

Since businesses have access to income that comes, not only from household expenditure, but also investment expenditures and government expenditures, they can sustain payments made to households in exchange for labour (and other factors of production) even though some household income is saved and some is paid as taxes.

It is only relatively recently—within the last century—that the potential for government to influence the state of the economy has been seriously explored. The great depression which began in the late 1920s and lasted through much of the 1930s led economists to ask what could be done to ease such dire circumstances. One possibility is to adjust taxation and government spending. In this context it is important to note that government spending does not all need to be financed by taxation; it is possible for governments to borrow (from the banks, or by issuing their own IOUs that may be bought by investors either in this country or elsewhere). By increasing its expenditure (without raising taxes) the government can stimulate economic activity. It can also stimulate economic activity by cutting taxes (without cutting its own expenditure)—in this case, households can keep more of their income to spend, thus providing a stimulus to the business sector. Towards the end of the 1930s, the advent of the second world war meant that many governments increased their spending, and this helped end the recession. That was a drastic and not altogether desirable cure.

The use of adjustments to taxation and government expenditure as a tool to regulate the level of activity in the economy as a whole is called fiscal policy—'fiscus' was the Latin term for the state treasury. In certain circumstances it can be an effective instrument, but there are limitations.

First, while it is certainly the case that government spending and taxation can move independently of one another, they can obviously only do so to the extent that the government can find sources of funding other than taxation to finance its spending. These alternative funding streams must come from somewhere—and ultimately from households' saving. If the government issues some IOUs (often called Treasury bills, gilts, or bonds), these are typically bought either directly by households or indirectly, as when a bank or other financial institution invests in them. This means that less is available for banks to plough into business investment. So using government expenditure to stimulate economic activity may be frustrated because, as government spending rises, so other injections into the business sector—notably investment—might fall.

This caveat arguably didn't apply in the 1930s because business investment had got stuck at low levels. In such circumstances, extra government spending could give the economy a kick that was not being provided by the private sector. Between 1929 and 1932, UK private sector investment fell by around 22%, due to a lack of confidence following the stock market crash at the start of this period. This shortfall could conceivably have been made good (earlier than it was) by government spending. But in general, it is important to examine the economy as a whole—including the government and banking sectors—and to avoid treating these sectors as things that exist completely independently of the productive sector that comprises business and households.

Secondly, the extent to which an economy can be stimulated by raising demand is necessarily limited by the capacity of the economy to produce. If there are idle resources—particularly if, as in the great depression, there are large pools of unemployed labour—it is possible to boost the economy by increasing demand. Supply will then respond—firms will hire more labour in order to produce more. But when the economy is already at full employment, this is not possible. To raise its output, a firm would have to increase its input of labour, but this would involve poaching workers from other firms (whose output would be reduced). To poach workers, the firm would have to increase the wages it pays, and to pay for this would need to raise also the prices it charges its customers. If all firms are playing the poaching game, the end result would be unchanged output (because there are no more workers in the system as a whole), but an escalation, or inflation, or wages and prices.

The difficulties of using tax and government spending as policy levers have led to alternative policies being favoured in many countries. In particular, interest rates have come to be regarded as the central policy tool for many governments. If interest rates are low, borrowers (such as firms wishing to invest in new productive capacity) are likely to take advantage of the low rates, and so this stimulates economic activity. At the same time, households are likely to limit their saving and spend more now since the incentive to save is low. If, on the other hand, interest rates are high, households and firms spend less and so economic activity tends to slow. We shall explore this relationship further in the coming chapters.

In times of recession, demand can be increased by the government either taxing less or spending more. Which would you prefer, and why?

Chapter 14
Unemployment—The Employers and the Employed

From Elizabeth Gaskell: Mary Barton

An order for coarse goods came in from a new foreign market. It was a large order, giving employment to all the mills engaged in that species of manufacture: but it was necessary to execute it speedily, and at as low prices as possible, as the masters had reason to believe a duplicate order had been sent to one of the continental manufacturing towns, where there were no restrictions on food, no taxes on building or machinery, and where consequently they dreaded that the goods could be made at a much lower price than they could afford them for; and that, by so acting and charging, the rival manufacturers would obtain undivided possession of the market. It was clearly their interest to buy cotton as cheaply, and to beat down wages as low as possible. And in the long run the interests of the workmen would have been thereby benefited. Distrust each other as they may, the employers and the employed must rise or fall together. There may be some difference as to chronology, none as to fact.

But the masters did not choose to make all these facts known. They stood upon being the masters, and that they had a right to order work at their own prices, and they believed that in the present depression of trade, and unemployment of hands, there would be no great difficulty in getting it done.

Mary Barton is the heroine of Elizabeth Gaskell's first novel, and she is romantically pursued by both Jem Wilson and the wealthy Harry Carson. The two young men fight, and when Harry is later found dead, Jem is falsely accused of his murder. An important subtext of the book's plot is the conditions of poverty in which many of the northern working class lived. While general trading conditions did not help, there was clearly concern among the workers that their employers were exploiting them. In those days, line managers may not have been able to send unpleasant emails at 3 o'clock in the morning, but there was no shortage of ways in which the bosses could make the bossed feel hard done by.

Unemployment hurts. Becoming unemployed reduces an individual's happiness by around 40%, and an increase of one percentage point in the overall unemployment

© The Author(s), under exclusive license to Springer Nature Switzerland AG 2023

G. Johnes, *Economics for Lovers of Literature*,
https://doi.org/10.1007/978-3-031-26486-3_14

rate reduces average happiness in a country by around 2%.[1] Yet it is quite a recent phenomenon. Before the industrial revolution, informal employment in agriculture (where workers might be hired to undertake very transient tasks—rather like the modern day gig economy) served as an alternative to the state of unemployment. So no protection against unemployment was necessary. With industrialisation, however, several things changed.

Arguably assisted by religious changes, the decline in belief in clerical authority, an increasing premium on self-confidence, and the consequent emergence of the protestant work ethic, the economic system evolved. Increasingly it became possible to invest in new production that generated employment, income and profit.

Workers relocated to urban areas where casual temporary employment opportunities were absent. Employers hired workers on a full-time basis because hiring and training staff to work in the new occupations was costly. Employment became binary—rather than varying the number of hours worked by each worker, it made sense for employers to vary the number of workers on their books. During a downturn, some workers would lose their jobs altogether. Data on unemployment started to be published late in the nineteenth century as trade unions responded to their members' plight by offering unemployment insurance; and official data were made available only as governments started to provide such insurance. What had been, in earlier times, a problem of underemployment because a problem of unemployment. Either of these problems reflects a shortfall of economic activity.

As we have seen, the overall level of economic activity fluctuates over time, a succession of downturns and recoveries being typical. During a downturn, unemployment rises, and during a recovery it falls. The increased unemployment as trading conditions worsen weaken workers' hand in wage bargaining, and so a downturn tends to be accompanied not only by greater joblessness but also by a dampening of wages. As Gaskell notes, the downturn should lead to lower goods prices too so that workers gain with one hand what they lose with the other—but, as she suspects, this mechanism often works imperfectly. Certainly, the binary nature of employment and unemployment means that the distribution of experience of a downturn across individuals is very uneven, with those thrown out of work suffering the most.

During a recovery, firms need to raise their output and, in order to achieve this, they need also to hire new workers. If the unemployment rate is high, they will probably be able to do this without having to raise the wage that they offer. But as the recovery continues it will become harder for them to find new workers. At some point, a firm wishing to increase its workforce will have to raise its wage offer in an attempt either to poach workers from other employers or to tempt people who have not had jobs heretofore into employment. To pay for these higher wages, the firm may need also to increase the prices that it charges on its finished products. When left unchecked, a recovery is characterised by a fall in unemployment (which is welcome) but also with an increase in price inflation (which is not). Conversely,

---

[1] Blanchflower, David G., David N.F. Bell, Alberto Montagnoli and Mirko Moro (2014) The happiness trade-off between unemployment and inflation, Journal of Money, Credit and Banking, 46, 117–141.

a recession is characterised by falling price inflation but also with an increase in unemployment. The good news is accompanied always by bad means that it is not for nothing that Thomas Carlyle called economics the 'dismal science'. And it is not for nothing that an exasperated President Harry Truman pleaded for someone to 'give me a one-handed economist'.

Conditions in the labour market do not affect just one firm in isolation. If one firm finds it must start paying higher wages to attract workers, then other firms are likely to be in much the same position. As firms have to fund their higher wage offers, workers may be frustrated to find that their increased pay does not allow them to buy more in the shops because prices have risen. Indeed, smart workers will take into account what they expect to happen to the general level of prices when they evaluate wage offers—if their expectations of price changes are formed rationally, taking into account all available information, workers should not make decisions about their response to wage offers that they subsequently regret because of what happens to prices. Ultimately, workers supply their labour on the basis not only of the wage offer, but also on the basis of what they expect to happen to price inflation.

In circumstances where unemployed workers expect a wage increase to be matched by an increase in the general price level, the hike in wages is unlikely to lead to a reduction in unemployment. Unemployed workers can see through the apparent wage increase—they can see it is not a real increase and that it cannot be converted to an improvement in the set of goods and services that they can afford to buy. Firms may want to expand their activities further—and indeed one firm might be able to at the expense of another—but in aggregate they cannot do so because they have come up against a very real constraint. The economy reaches a point when it is working at full capacity. Any further expansion of the economy would result in price inflation, but would not enable more stuff to be produced, and would not enable people, in any real sense, to become better off. Ultimately, at any point in time, there is a limit to what we can produce. To produce more would require us, rather tautologically, to become more productive.

Mary Barton is set in northern England during the years of recession following the panic of 1837—which began as improved infrastructure in America led to a collapse in cotton prices and the subsequent failure of American debtors to repay loans. Workers tried to protect their employment status by accepting wage cuts—average wages fell about 5% from around 3 shillings and a penny per day to around 2 shillings and 11 pence between 1837 and 1840[2]—this was not sufficient to prevent a rise in unemployment from 7½ to 10%.[3] As Mrs Gaskell points out, and as Mandeville's fable of the bees suggests, there should be a synergy between the interests of the manufacturers and those of the workmen. But, in light of their experience during this recession, it is perhaps not surprising that these workers suspected that their employers were exploiting them.

A job is an institutional arrangement—a bundling together of tasks that employers and employees expect to remain stable over a long period of time. If

---

[2] https://bit.ly/3ueIESx.

[3] https://bit.ly/3sHw1iF.

technology changes in a way that destabilises this bundling, a job might become redundant. No job lasts forever, but some are more stable than others. What, in your view, are the protections that workers need in order to ensure that they have 'good work'?

Chapter 15
Monetary Policy—Interesting Times

From William Makepeace Thackeray: The Newcomes

The Bundelcund Bank, which had been established for four years, had now grown to be one of the most flourishing commercial institutions in Bengal. Founded, as the prospectus announced, at a time when all private credit was shaken by the failure of the great Agency Houses, of which the downfall had carried dismay and ruin throughout the Presidency, the B. B. had been established on the only sound principle of commercial prosperity—that is association. The native capitalists, headed by the great firm of Rummun Loll and Co., of Calcutta, had largely embarked in the B. B., and the officers of the two services and the European mercantile body of Calcutta had been invited to take shares in an institution which, to merchants, native and English, civilian and military men, was alike advantageous and indispensable. How many young men of the latter services had been crippled for life by the ruinous cost of agencies, of which the profits to the agents themselves were so enormous! The shareholders of the B. B. were their own agents; and the greatest capitalist in India as well as the youngest ensign in the service might invest at the largest and safest premium, and borrow at the smallest interest, by becoming according to his means, a shareholder in the B. B.

The Newcomes is, after a fashion, a sequel to Thackeray's most popular novel, Vanity Fair—at least inasmuch as some of the characters from Vanity Fair make cameo appearances in the later book. It follows two generations of central characters over a long period and cast in multiple locations across the world. Over time, the Newcomes acquire wealth and status through a combination of their banking interests and marrying into money. While I was reading this book, I had a conversation with an elderly relative who regaled me with all sorts of fanciful stories about the source of wealth of some of our senior politicians. The ones she liked were fine. Some of the others—if she was to be believed—were child-eating senicidists. Call me naïve, but I'll call her cynical! The Newcomes is a long, rambling book, initially written in serial form—and it shows. Think Tristram Shandy but twice as long and

© The Author(s), under exclusive license to Springer Nature Switzerland AG 2023
G. Johnes, *Economics for Lovers of Literature*,
https://doi.org/10.1007/978-3-031-26486-3_15

lacking the humour. Mercifully, it improves as it progresses, and by the end it is a genuine page-turner.

Investing at the largest premium and borrowing at the smallest interest certainly sounds like a good deal. Banks accept deposits from people and organisations that want to save. They use some of these deposits to make loans to other people and organisations that want to borrow. In so doing, they necessarily gamble that depositors will only ever want to withdraw a relatively small proportion of their deposits at any one time. This gamble introduces a vulnerability—and a recurring theme in The Newcomes concerns the attempts of the egregious Barnes Newcome to exploit this vulnerability to threaten the Bundelcund bank. Indeed, excessive risky lending (including to one of its own auditors) proves to have been the cause of the bank's demise. Currently UK banks manage vulnerability by holding at least 12½% of whatever is deposited as a reserve—that is, they do not lend this out. The banks then offer interest (or a premium) to depositors as an incentive for them to save; meanwhile, they charge interest to borrowers—and this is the source of the banks' income. There is typically a wedge between the interest rates charged for borrowing and those offered for saving; this wedge is needed partly because the bank cannot risk lending out everything that it holds as deposits, and partly in order that the bank can fund its own costs of operation and make a profit. As interest rates rise, so saving becomes more attractive and borrowing becomes less so. This is an important observation, not least because it means that interest rates have the potential to be used as a tool in regulating the overall level of economic activity.

On any one day, it is possible (and indeed highly likely) that depositors at a bank might wish to withdraw more funds than the bank has available. When this happens, the bank must borrow in order to tide it over to the next day. The central bank—which is the organisation responsible for regulating the supply of money in an economy—makes overnight and other short-term loans available to cover such needs. The rate of interest that the central bank charges on these loans are hugely influential in setting the interest rates that banks charge on loans that they make to businesses and other clients. On a regular basis, every few weeks, the central bank announces its target rate of interest. The central bank has a dominant position in the market, and so the announcement is often in itself sufficient to set the interest rate; otherwise, the central bank may trade in securities in such a way as to ensure that its target is met.

A high rate of interest discourages borrowing. This means that companies are less likely to invest in new productive capacity—new machinery, new buildings, or land—when interest rates are relatively high. And because high-interest rates discourage borrowing, they also tend to reduce spending by consumers. So the overall level of demand in the economy is reduced, and this puts downward pressure on prices. Raising interest rates can therefore be a useful policy tool if the aim is to reduce price inflation.

A low rate of interest, meanwhile, encourages borrowing by businesses and consumers. It increases demand. Lowering interest rates can be a useful policy tool if the economy is performing sluggishly—it can provide a boost to the output produced in the economy as a whole, and so can stimulate national income and increase employment.

Whenever someone chooses to hold their assets in the form of money (rather than, say, in an interest-bearing bank account), they are paying for their convenience by sacrificing interest payments. So the interest rate may be interpreted as being the price of money. For this reason, the central bank's manipulation of the interest rate is referred to as an example of monetary policy. Policies of this kind are discretionary in the sense that the central bank chooses to raise or lower the interest rate. Nevertheless, the link between the policy tool—the interest rate—and economic outcomes—national income, unemployment, price inflation—suggests that we can think of monetary policy in terms of a rule of thumb. If inflation is high and the authorities want to cut it, they should increase interest rates. If, on the other hand, inflation is low and unemployment is high, they should cut interest rates. We'll have more to say about this rule of thumb in a later chapter.

It is worth pausing for a moment to give more consideration to the concept of money. We might all think we would like more money, but that is not really the case. Very often we would be better off holding our assets in a form other than money—in land, or in stocks and shares, or simply in a bank account that offers a good rate of interest. However, money does provide a valuable service in that it facilitates trade. Indeed it would be hard to imagine a functioning economy without money. A characteristic of any trade is that the seller gives something to the buyer in exchange for something that the buyer gives to the seller. In the absence of money, they would have to negotiate a barter, directly exchanging goods and services for other goods and services. If I were to sell you this book on such a basis, I might agree with one reader that he would come and clean my house, I might agree with another reader that she would give me her bike, and I might agree with a third reader that he would drive me to and from the nearest city. All of this negotiation would be so time-consuming, it would severely curtail the amount of genuinely productive activity that goes on. By acting as a common currency, money finesses all of this.

Rather disconcertingly, this means that anything that is capable of doing what money does can be considered to be money. Money does not have to have any intrinsic value. This is why so much money is really only paper. A £50 note is worth £50 only because everybody accepts that it is worth £50—I can use it to pay you, and you will accept it because you know that other people would accept it as payment from you. Cigarettes were used as a form of money in prisoner of war camps because they are very portable (so can be used as a medium of exchange), they are an ideal unit of account (they're all the same size), and they work well as a store of value (they don't melt like ice cream). The central bank in an economy is responsible for ensuring that there is enough money in circulation to meet the needs of the economy. It is responsible for printing notes and minting coins, but its control of the stock of money in the economy is exercised through its purchases and sales of financial assets. If the central bank buys securities from commercial banks, it puts money into the financial system. If it sells securities—and typically it will need to offer securities at a higher interest rate in order to do this—it reduces the amount of money in the system.

The central bank must also make sure that it does not allow the amount of money in the economy to grow too quickly. An excess of money would be accompanied by low-interest rates, and this would likely lead to high levels of borrowing by businesses and consumers, raising the overall level of demand for goods and services. But since there are limits to how much of these goods and services can be produced, this extra demand would push prices up. Too rapid a growth in the money stock in an economy generates price inflation. So, in setting interest rates and regulating the supply of money in the economy, the central bank faces a delicate balancing act.

Governments have frequently used interest rate policy to try to regulate the level of demand in the economy—for example by setting a target rate of price inflation, and requiring the central bank to raise or lower interest rates in an attempt at hitting this target. Other than inflation, what other measures of economic performance do you think governments should target, and what policy tools do you think might be used to meet those objectives?

Chapter 16
Modern Models of the Macroeconomy—From Small Things, Big Things Come

From James Barrie: The Little White Bird

If you ask your mother whether she knew about Peter Pan when she was a little girl she will say, "Why, of course, I did, child", and if you ask her whether he rode on a goat in those days she will say, "What a foolish question to ask; certainly he did". Then if you ask your grandmother whether she knew about Peter Pan when she was a girl, she also says, "Why, of course, I did, child", but if you ask her whether he rode on a goat in those days, she says she never heard of his having a goat. Perhaps she has forgotten, just as she sometimes forgets your name and calls you Mildred, which is your mother's name. Still, she could hardly forget such an important thing as the goat. Therefore there was no goat when your grandmother was a little girl. This shows that, in telling the story of Peter Pan, to begin with the goat (as most people do) is as silly as to put on your jacket before your vest.

Of course, it also shows that Peter is ever so old, but he is really always the same age, so that does not matter in the least. His age is one week, and though he was born so long ago he has never had a birthday, nor is there the slightest chance of his ever having one. The reason is that he escaped from being a human when he was seven days' old; he escaped by the window and flew back to the Kensington Gardens.

If you think he was the only baby who ever wanted to escape, it shows how completely you have forgotten your own young days. When David heard this story first he was quite certain that he had never tried to escape, but I told him to think back hard, pressing his hands to his temples, and when he had done this hard, and even harder, he distinctly remembered a youthful desire to return to the tree-tops, and with that memory came others, as that he had lain in bed planning to escape as soon as his mother was asleep, and how she had once caught him half-way up the chimney. All children could have such recollections if they would press their hands hard to their temples, for, having been birds

G. Johnes, *Economics for Lovers of Literature*,
https://doi.org/10.1007/978-3-031-26486-3_16

before they were human, they are naturally a little wild during the first few weeks, and very itchy at the shoulders, where their wings used to be.

Peter Pan was a character in Barrie's book The Little White Bird before he became the subject of a play and later a novel for children. The character may have been inspired by Barrie's brother who, having died at a young age, never grew old. The book's theme concerns the passage of time and changing relationships, with the character of Peter Pan providing a counterpoint. To be honest, I found this to be a profoundly uncomfortable read. It is creepy and voyeuristic, and there are sinister undercurrents of psychological abuse and paedophilia. But while much the book is far from innocent, there is a fantastic and delightful book within the book that tells the story of Peter Pan. This character is Allais important in our consideration of the overall economy because, in common with the economy, he straddles time. Economic outcomes and decisions in one period are influenced both by what has happened before and by what is expected to happen in the future.

The modern approach to analysing the economy as a whole takes advantage of computer technology to mimic sophisticated behaviour patterns among households, businesses and government. In each 'block', economic decision-makers are seeking to optimise their objectives dynamically (that is, over a long period of time, not just at one instant), while being bombarded by random surprise events (that is, they are presented with a stochastic scenario at each point in time), and subject to constraints.

In the household block, the typical household seeks to maximise its utility by working to secure an income, and by spending or saving this income. Other things being equal, it will choose to work intensively, particularly when the returns to work are high; at other times it might choose to produce less and to enjoy more leisure. The household will usually choose to consume more at times when the interest rate is low (thus making saving less attractive) and when price inflation is expected to rise (so that it can take advantage of low current prices that are soon set to increase). The household's ability to consume depends in part on wealth that it has accumulated through savings in the past, and its desire to consume depends in part on price increases that it expects to happen in the future—so its decisions are truly dynamic. The way in which households form expectations of the future time path of prices is particularly interesting; obviously, their forecasts can be wrong—forecasts always are—but persistent systematic errors should not be made. Sensible behaviour entails using all available information in formulating these expectations, and this means that the process of making predictions about prices should correct for any systematic mistakes that have been made in the past. In this respect, households have rational expectations. This is an important point, because it makes possible a mathematical representation of expectations that is consistent with the system that is being analysed.

In the business block, the typical firm wishes to maximise its stream of future profit. In so doing, it faces a number of constraints concerning the demand for its product (and hence prices) and concerning labour supply (and hence wages). If the firm wishes to increase its output, it can do so by increasing wages—this allows it to increase labour employment, so it can produce more. But the increase in wages has a knock-on effect on prices. Assuming imperfect competition, prices may be set as a mark-up on wages. So increased supply implies both a rise in wages and a rise in prices. The most general formulations of business behaviour enshrine some inertia into the way in which prices (and wages) change over time—allowing gradual adjustment provides a richer set of possible outcomes than does an insistence that adjustment should be instantaneous (simply because instantaneous adjustment then becomes just a special case). A common specification is to allow the firm to change only a fraction of its prices in any one period. The key thing to note about the business block is thus that it provides a relationship between employment, wages and prices.[1]

In the government block, policy-makers are assumed to seek stability in the economy by adjusting the interest rate. Noting that a relatively high-interest rate reduces demand (because households choose to save more), policy-makers will raise the interest rate when price inflation is high (in an attempt to reduce demand and hence put downward pressure on prices), and they will reduce it when price inflation is low.[2]

Bringing together the household, business and government blocks entails constructing a rather sophisticated system, and solving for values of key variables involves computationally intensive numerical methods. This being the case, modern analysis of such a complex economy does not yield simple rules of thumb. But it does offer a means of studying an economy that ensures logical consistency in that decision-makers in households, businesses and governments are all behaving rationally in pursuit of their objectives. Systems of this kind are often referred to as dynamic stochastic general equilibrium, or DSGE, models. They have come to be very widely used as tools of policy evaluation and forecasting within government agencies.

Logical consistency is fine as far as it goes. But, as we saw in Chapter 11, individuals do not always behave in the ways that might be expected if they were always to pursue a consistent set of objectives. People's responses to a particular situation often depend on the framing of that situation. So the attempt to use the assumption of rational behaviour as a means either of explaining the past or predicting the future has obvious limitations. It provides a good starting point. Perhaps, in future, a better starting point will be offered by taking more fully into account the way in which people actually make their decisions.

Consider what is meant by 'rational expectations'—the idea that people base their expectations of what will happen in the future on all available information. How do such expectations square with what we have learned about information deficiencies? And with what we have learned about how people actually behave?

---

[1] This is sometimes described as a Phillips curve, in honour of the pioneering work of Bill Phillips—see A.W. Phillips (1958) The relation between unemployment and the rate of change of money wage rates in the United Kingdom, 1861–1957, Economica, 25, 283–299.

[2] This type of policy is sometimes described as a Taylor rule, in honour of the work of John Taylor—see J.B. Taylor (1993) Discretion versus policy rules in practice, Carnegie-Rochester Conference Series on Public Policy, 39, 195–214.

Chapter 17
Growth—Growing Pains

From Anthony Trollope: Phineas Finn

If we do have representation, let the representative assembly be like the people, whatever else may be its virtues,—and whatever else its vices.

Another great authority has told us that our House of Commons should be the mirror of the people. I say, not its mirror, but its miniature. And let the artist be careful to put in every line of the expression of that ever-moving face. To do this is a great work, and the artist must know his trade well. In America the work has been done with so coarse a hand that nothing is shown in the picture but the broad, plain, unspeaking outline of the face. As you look from the represented to the representation you cannot but acknowledge the likeness;—but there is in that portrait more of the body than of the mind. The true portrait should represent more than the body. With us, hitherto, there have been snatches of the countenance of the nation which have been inimitable,—a turn of the eye here and a curl of the lip there, which have seemed to denote a power almost divine. There have been marvels on the canvas so beautiful that one approaches the work of remodelling it with awe. But not only is the picture imperfect,—a thing of snatches,—but with years it becomes less and still less like its original.

The necessity for remodelling it is imperative, and we shall be cowards if we decline the work. But let us be specially careful to retain as much as possible of those lines which we all acknowledge to be so faithfully representative of our nation. To give to a bare numerical majority of the people that power which the numerical majority has in the United States, would not be to achieve representation. The nation as it now exists would not be known by such a portrait;—but neither can it now be known by that which exists. It seems to me that they who are adverse to change, looking back with an unmeasured respect on what our old Parliaments have done for us, ignore the majestic growth of the English people, and forget the present in their worship of the past. They think that we must be what we were,—at any rate, what we were thirty years since. They have not, perhaps, gone into the houses of artisans, or, if there, they have not looked into

© The Author(s), under exclusive license to Springer Nature Switzerland AG 2023
G. Johnes, *Economics for Lovers of Literature*,
https://doi.org/10.1007/978-3-031-26486-3_17

the breasts of the men. With population vice has increased, and these politicians, with ears but no eyes, hear of drunkenness and sin and ignorance. And then they declare to themselves that this wicked, half-barbarous, idle people should be controlled and not represented. A wicked, half-barbarous, idle people may be controlled;—but not a people thoughtful, educated, and industrious. We must look to it that we do not endeavour to carry our control beyond the wickedness and the barbarity, and that we be ready to submit to control from thoughtfulness and industry.

In 1974 my parents bought our first colour TV. They did so in order to watch, in its full glory, a BBC series called The Pallisers. The series was based on novels by Anthony Trollope. Until then these works had often been referred to as the Parliamentary Novels (but they have since more commonly been called the Palliser novels). Phineas Finn concerns the story of an Irishman from a modest background who rises through the political ranks—aided in part by his connections and a fortuitous incident in which he becomes a hero. He served in the Treasury at the time when Plantagenet Palliser was Chancellor of the Exchequer. Political themes (notably concerning land reform and parliamentary representation) provide important background, though Finn's romantic entanglements (and they really are tangled) represent the core of the plot.

The flow of incomes and expenditures between households and businesses forms the cornerstone of our thinking about how the economy as a whole performs. There are times when the economy performs better than others, and, as we have seen, there may be a role for government to play in moderating these fluctuations. But the fundamental lesson of the circular flow of income is this: variation in the national income comes about as a result of variation in what is produced. If, as a nation, we wish to become richer, we can do so only by producing more.

A number of mechanisms can help workers to produce more in each hour that they work. One is to have the tools for the job. Finding, and using, the right mix of labour and machinery allows the labour to be used productively. Improving the quality of machinery through innovation serves to make labour more productive. Improving processes—making the management of organisations slicker and more efficient—likewise makes labour more productive. If machines can carry more of the load, a given amount of labour can produce more.

The relationship between humans and machines is not the only thing that is important in making us more productive, though. As Joshua Monk wrote to Phineas Finn, having a population that is 'thoughtful, educated and industrious' is critical. More highly educated workers tend to be more productive. A key route to securing economic growth is therefore to improve educational attainment, thereby augmenting the stock of human capital in an economy. This being the case, it is not surprising to find that statistical analyses seeking to establish the link between economic growth and a country's stocks of capital and labour are much improved by modifying the way in which labour is measured so that it takes into account the 'quality' of labour.

Trade is another factor that influences economic growth in the long run. Countries that encourage free trade with other countries, imposing few tariffs and other trade barriers, tend, other things being equal, to grow relatively quickly. In recent decades the dramatic economic development of major countries such as China and India has followed major moves towards trade liberalisation—notably, China's open door policy introduced in 1978, and India's tariff reforms begun in 1991. The removal of barriers allows the trades that ought to be made to happen, with an overall gain in efficiency.

Numerous other factors influence economic growth. For obvious reasons, businesses are relatively likely to invest in economies characterised by a stable political system and with an absence of corruption, and by enhancing the productivity of labour this investment feeds through to growth. Conflict is—again for obvious reasons—anathema to growth.

In recent decades, economic growth has served to bring many millions of people out of poverty. World Bank estimates suggest that, while in 1981, more than 40% of the world's population lived in extreme poverty, the corresponding figure now is well below 10%. This is a stunning achievement and should be regarded as a (very) good thing.

There is, however, a downside to economic growth. Recall that production involves converting inputs into outputs. Inputs are resources, and these resources may be renewable immediately, quickly, slowly, or not at all. Where the resources are exhaustible, production can be problematic. Producing stuff now imposes a negative spillover effect on future generations. As we saw in Chapter 8, spillover effects of this kind need to be mitigated.

In other cases, a byproduct of production maybe pollution. This is an undesirable output. Again, this is a negative spillover effect of the production process, and again it needs to be mitigated.

Neither the use of exhaustible resources nor the production of pollutants means that economic growth in itself is a bad thing. Some forms of production use only renewables and do not pollute at all. But clearly, measures need to be in place to discourage harmful production and to encourage clean production. If property rights (including the right of future generations to a clean environment) are not well enough defined to ensure that these aims are secured by market forces, then government intervention may be necessary.

Neither Plantagenet Palliser nor Phineas Finn had access to sophisticated DSGE methods; much of our present day understanding of how the economy works had yet to be developed. Likewise, concerns about environmental issues had yet to surface. Economic growth offered a route out of poverty and into prosperity, and the long run determinants of such growth—investment in physical and human capital, and trade—were well understood. Those investments continue so that we can enjoy growth into the future. And, as we enjoy the prosperity we currently have, we stand on the shoulders of giants.

What are the limits to growth?

Index

© The Editor(s) (if applicable) and The Author(s), under exclusive license
to Springer Nature Switzerland AG 2023
G. Johnes, *Economics for Lovers of Literature*,
https://doi.org/10.1007/978-3-031-26486-3